Still Pitching

*Musings from the Mound
and the Microphone*

Jim Kaat

with Phil Pepe

TRIUMPH
B O O K S
CHICAGO

Library of Congress Cataloging-in-Publication Data

Kaat, Jim.
    Still pitching : musings from the mound and the microphone / Jim Kaat with Phil Pepe.
        p. cm.
    Includes index.
    ISBN 1-57243-518-6 (hard)
        1. Kaat, Jim. 2. Baseball players—United States—Biography. 3. Sportscasters—United States—Biography. I. Pepe, Phil. II. Title.

GV865.K22 A3 2003
796.357'092—dc21
[B]
                                                              2002040920

This book is available in quantity at special discounts for your group or organization. For further information, contact:
Triumph Books
601 South LaSalle Street
Suite 500
Chicago, Illinois 60605
(312) 939-3330
Fax (312) 663-3557

Printed in the United States of America
ISBN 1-57243-518-6
Interior design by Patricia Frey
All photos are courtesy of the personal collection of Jim Kaat except where otherwise noted.

This book is dedicated to the memory of my dad, John Kaat, known as "Mr. Baseball" in Zeeland, Michigan, who kindled my interest in baseball when I was seven with stories about Lefty Grove and Connie Mack and took me to my first game at Briggs Stadium, Detroit, in 1946. He was the perfect dad for an athlete. He never pushed me too hard, always pointed out who helped me in my successful games, and was quick to say, "There'll be another day," after my bad ones. He was tough, but tender. Thanks, Dad.

And to Mary Ann Montanaro, the most brilliant and caring woman I've ever met.

I would also like to acknowledge my son Jim, who sent me this wonderful note after my final year of eligibility for the Hall of Fame:

Hi, Dad. I just want to take a moment to congratulate you on your 130 writer votes. I know it does not matter to you and you never expressed a real concern, but if it means anything to you, you will always be a Hall of Famer in my book. And one other thing, Dad, I want you to remember that scene from the movie The Natural. *Roy Hobbs, played by Robert Redford, asks Max Mercy, a New York sportswriter played by Bob Duvall, "Did you ever play the game, Max?" His answer: "No, I never did, but I'm here to protect this game." And Roy says, "Whose game, Max?" And after an awkward pause, Max says, "Either way, Roy, hero or goat, you are going to make me a great story." And I say this to you because in the future, when your peers on the Veterans Committee vote you into the Hall of Fame, that will be the true measure of your success. Because, in the end, writers write—that is all they do well—and players play, and there is no higher accomplishment than the ultimate respect from your peers. I love you, Dad.*

7/03

Contents

Foreword

So my good friend Jim Kaat has written a book. Knowing Jimmy as I have for almost 30 years, I was certain his book would comprise some of the same qualities he employed as a pitcher, and still employs as a television broadcaster/analyst: it would be thorough, informative, insightful, and a quick read.

As players we were contemporaries, but not frequent competitors, since he spent most of his career in the American League and I spent all of mine in the National League. I did face him a few times. I hit a home run off him in spring training, which was about the extent of my success against him.

As a pitcher, Kitty was a thorn in hitters' sides. You'd look at him and know that behind that poker face he was thinking of ways to beat you. I always admired Kitty's competitiveness and his ability to make adjustments as he wended his way through the various stages of his career, a career that spanned an astonishing 25 years.

There was never anything fancy about Jimmy on the mound. He just came at you and threw strikes, and he worked quickly and kept hitters off balance. You had to be ready to hit when he was pitching.

His approach to his current role as a broadcaster/analyst is not unlike his approach to pitching. He doesn't talk over people's heads. He comes right at you with nothing fancy.

Jim was there when I arrived with the Yankees in 1996. I had the opportunity to observe his work first-hand. As an analyst, he's not one-dimensional. He utilizes all the information and experience he gathered from his many years in baseball. He's never lost the enthusiasm for the game that he had when he first started broadcasting. He has continued to work at his job. Kitty never wanted to be just OK as a broadcaster. He wanted to be better than that—and he is.

When Jim Kaat walks into my office he's so knowledgeable, so direct and aboveboard, that I feel an obligation to give him information because of who he is and what he has accomplished. The next thing I know, somebody is coming to me and saying, "Did you hear what Jim Kaat said on television? . . ."

I got to see another side of Jim when we were both active with the Major League Players Association. I found him to be a man of strong dedication and commitment. And through the years, I came to learn that when Jim Kaat talks—or writes—you pay attention because he always has something interesting, something thought provoking, and something instructive to say.

—Joe Torre
Bronx, New York

Preface

His career spanned three commissioners, four decades, five teams in six cities, and seven presidential administrations, from Eisenhower to Reagan. He played with eight Hall of Famers and for 15 managers.

He pitched to Ted Williams and Darryl Strawberry, Yogi Berra and his son Dale, and Maury Wills and his son Bump. And he gave up home runs to Aaron and Zisk.

In his first major league season, there were eight teams in each league, and some still traveled by train. In his last major league season, there were 26 teams. He had witnessed 10 new teams enter through expansion and three franchise relocations.

When he left the game as an active player (he never formally announced his retirement and still is available to any team in need of a crafty, veteran, southpaw), he had played more seasons than any other player in the history of modern major league baseball: 25; he had appeared in 898 games, pitched 4,528 innings, won 283 games, struck out 2,461 batters, walked 1,083, pitched 180 complete games and 31 shutouts, and won 16 Gold Gloves for his defensive prowess.

James Lee (Jim) Kaat clearly has been a man for all seasons.

His involvement in major league baseball continues. After his playing career ended, Kaat turned to broadcasting, and he is approaching half a century in baseball. A keen observer and a renowned student of baseball, he has been following the game for almost 60 years.

Today, he is a television broadcaster/analyst for New York Yankees games, a voice of reason and responsibility, among the most astute observers of baseball's passing scene, and an aficionado of the theories and techniques of pitching. Jim Kaat is an opinionated and outspoken critic of those who have desecrated this great game, yet he remains reverent and respectful of the game he loves and of those who play it and have played it.

Introduction

Sometimes when I'm working a little too late in the day and there's an afternoon Yankees game on, I turn on the TV and watch, or, more accurately, listen, varying my attention based on the degree of activity on the field as I finish up the day's work. It's a nice way to cushion the end of a workday, and I have a genuine excuse for it as well, since I am now an official columnist for ESPN's website. When I tuned in last summer I gradually picked up on what was an extraordinary ongoing pitching clinic being conducted by Jim Kaat, a former pitcher with the Senators, the Twins, the White Sox, the Phillies, the Yankees, and the Cardinals. It was a genuine, and fascinating, pleasure. At a certain point it struck me that, even though I am a lifelong baseball fan, there is still much for me to learn about the game. That knowledge makes me love the game even more.

This was of course more than just a pitching clinic—because a pitching clinic is by its nature a hitting clinic as well. It was great fun, and listening to Jim Kaat gradually pulled me away from my work. After a few weeks I wrote in my ESPN column that, in what was a damaged year in baseball, one in which the threat of a strike hung over most of the season, Kaat was my hero because he seemed to reflect what the game is all about. Gradually it struck me that I was listening to one of the best broadcasters I had ever heard.

Here's what I like about listening to Jim Kaat: he has a rare knowledge of the game, a knowledge that he passes on without any pretension and makes very accessible. He has opinions, and they are *his* opinions—that is, his judgment is obviously independent (which I suspect reflects his independence as a man), and his opinions do not seem to be tailored to the needs and uses of the home team. He also demonstrates an admirable lack of self-promotion, something very rare in big-time sports these days, and he seems to realize that he is there to help the fans appreciate the game rather than to sell himself. Finally, he has a respect for the intelligence of his audience—he is not, as so often happens these days, someone who thinks he can manipulate the audience and use his talents for his own career advantage. That last is no small virtue in any form of broadcast media.

These virtues are old-fashioned. That same nature comes through in this memoir: that is, what Kaat sounds like on the air is who he really is. I am pleased by this. I have felt for years that I have a stake in Jim Kaat's career because, in a broad sense, we came up to the big leagues together. We were both down in Tennessee in 1959. He was with the Chattanooga Lookouts, a Double A Washington Senators farm club—that's how long ago it was, Washington still had a baseball team—and I was a young, very ambitious reporter for the Nashville *Tennessean*, which was arguably the best nonnational newspaper in the country at the time. He made cameo end-of-the-season appearances with the big club in 1959 and 1960 and landed in Washington for good in 1961; by chance I left the *Tennessean* in late 1960, after five years in the South, and went to the Washington bureau of *The New York Times* a few days before John Kennedy's inauguration in January 1961. In 1959, as he mentions in this memoir, Kaat struck out 19 Nashville batters; I was very aware of that game at the time. So I've been watching him, it seems to me, for a long time.

One of the interesting facets of this memoir is how old-fashioned, or perhaps more accurately, how unmodern, it is. The man, his background, and his values are all of a piece. He seems the ultimate traditionalist, the product of a hard-working Dutch-American family from a politically conservative region of Michigan. His people do not complain about life; instead, they accept the complexities of fate. The young Jim Kaat loved baseball as a boy—one of his strengths as a broadcaster, I think, is that he's still a fan at heart—and was encouraged by his father to play as much ball as he could. He did, and he was good, but his physical growth came slowly, and he was still quite small when he finished high school (though he would eventually be almost 6'5"). With no scholarship offers to consider Jim enrolled at Hope College, a religiously centered school that was located near his home. He went there, did well, and drew the interest of scouts.

Here we come upon the defining part of the book—and the defining part of what makes Jim Kaat who he is. The Senators were interested in him and offered him a bonus of $4,000 if he would agree to sign in 1957. That was a decent wage in those days—as I recall, it was almost exactly what I made that year with my paper, around $80 a week. By chance the Chicago White Sox were also interested and offered him a bonus of $25,000, a huge amount of money, especially for a family like his. As he notes, it was the equivalent of what his father, John Kaat, made in *seven years* working at a difficult job in the local turkey hatchery.

It was a difficult decision for Jim, easily dazzled by the offer and Chicago's interest—but it was an easy choice for John Kaat. He knew the rules of baseball, knew that if a player received a bonus over $4,000 he had to spend two years on the major league roster, and that therefore his learning curve was likely to be badly damaged. He knew the names of all the bonus baby pitchers who had not panned out. And he had tremendous faith in his son and an old-fashioned belief that if Jim went out and worked hard, and he was really supposed to be a big league pitcher, then it would happen. And if, on the other hand, he went out and worked hard and still didn't make it, at least they would have the satisfaction of knowing they did it the right way. Reading about that time in Jim's life, it is obvious that Kaat is still moved by his father's decision.

Not surprisingly, Kaat improved year by year, became a student of the game, impressed his varying minor league managers with his commitment, and became physically stronger as well. Cookie Lavagetto, who dealt with him as a representative of the Washington organization early on, predicted that he would make the big club in three years, and he made it in two and a half instead. But he also remembered the values of the way he did it, the value of an apprenticeship and learning how to pitch at just the proper pace.

In this book Kaat tells of a number of superstar prospects who were signed at a very high figure and were put on too fast a track with too much pressure on them. He tells the story of Todd Van Poppel, a Texas phenom said to be the next Nolan Ryan, who was represented by the prominent agent Scott Boras. Van Poppel signed a contract that guaranteed he would be on the major league roster in a very short time. For all of the wealth of his first contract—peanuts compared to what he might have earned if he had reached his full potential—Van Poppel never quite made it big, and would have been better off being represented by John Kaat instead of Boras.

Well, Jim Kaat is like his father, and so is this book; it's full of the reflections of a an old-fashioned man who beat all the odds, made the majors in a short time, stayed there for 25 years, and won 283 games. All in all a man worth listening to.

—David Halberstam

CHAPTER **1**

An Age-Old Story

I was looking forward to the All-Star break. A little golf, some rest and relaxation, and then back to what I was certain was going to be another close, exciting race in the National League East.

It was 1983, and I was a member of the St. Louis Cardinals, my fifth major league team. We had won the World Series the year before. We had finished three games ahead of the Philadelphia Phillies in the National League East, our division, beat Joe Torre's Atlanta Braves three straight in the National League Championship Series, then won the World Series from the Milwaukee Brewers in seven games by taking the last two games in St. Louis.

I had had a decent year. Pitching almost exclusively in relief, I was 5–3 with two saves.

Now I was in my fourth season with the Cardinals, longer than I had been with any team since the Twins. I hadn't pitched much in the first half—just 34⅔ innings in 24 games, no record, no saves, but

1

a 3.89 earned run average. And I was feeling pretty good about the second half, for the team and for myself.

We had gotten off to a slow start, but by the break, we were in the thick of the NL East race and we had some good veteran players—George Hendrick, Tommy Herr, Ozzie Smith, Willie McGee, Darrell Porter, an excellent pitching staff with Bob Forsch, Joaquin Andujar, John Stuper, Dave LaPoint, and, in my opinion, the best closer in the game, Bruce Sutter—pretty much the same cast that had won the World Series. And we had Whitey Herzog, a manager with a knack for getting the most out of the talent he had.

I had been sold by the Yankees to the Cardinals early in the 1980 season. When I arrived, Ken Boyer was the Cardinals manager, but after I was there a little more than a month, Boyer was fired and Herzog was brought in.

I had played against Whitey when he managed, very successfully I might add, in Texas and Kansas City. Herzog was the most brilliant and the brightest manager I ever played for. The way he used me, and the way he ran a game, he was the best.

He was the manager in St. Louis for about two months when he was made general manager, so he left the field and went up to the front office and Red Schoendienst, the great Cardinals' Hall of Fame second baseman, took over for the remainder of the season. It was just an interim position for Schoendienst, who had managed the Cardinals for 12 years and had won two pennants and one World Series with those great Cardinals teams in the late sixties.

When the 1980 season ended, the organization announced that Herzog would serve as both field manager and general manager, so I would deal with Whitey when it came time to negotiate a new contract. I didn't have an agent. I always did all my own negotiations. With Whitey, it was a simple process. I'd go to Herzog at the end of

Make It Move

The best pitching advice I can give young pitchers is to learn to throw strikes with your fastball. I had a young pitcher named Andy McGaffigan in Cincinnati who boasted that he had four pitches. I said, "How many of them can you throw for strikes on 3–2 in a clutch situation? If you can't throw all four for strikes, maybe you have only one pitch."

I'd take him to the bullpen and say, "Throw 10 fastballs. See how many you can throw in the strike zone. I don't care if you hit the corner. I want strikes." Sometimes he'd throw four or five for strikes and I'd tell him, "If you're just trying to throw strikes and you can't throw more than four or five in the strike zone, what are you doing trying to hit corners?"

Pitching starts with being able to throw a fastball for strikes 90 percent of the time. Everything works off that.

People have asked me when a kid should start throwing curveballs. I don't know if there's any set age. When I was little, I didn't throw hard, so early on I started learning how to curve the ball. That may not be the proper advice to give a youngster, but to me it's more important for a youngster to learn *how* to throw a curveball, not *when*. The key to learning to throw a breaking ball is to use your wrist, not your elbow. Young pitchers hurt their arms by throwing with their elbow instead of using the wrist and finger pressure.

Greg Maddux is one pitcher today who still puts a lot of emphasis on finger pressure, spin, and the rotation of the ball. Everybody today tends to be power-conscious. In my day, pitchers were more spin-conscious. Make it move. Make it do this, make it do that.

the season and ask him, "What do you think? Do you think I can still pitch? You want me back?"

"Yeah," he'd say. "I think you can still do it."

Then we'd talk money. He'd say, "What were you making last year, $135,000? What do you think you ought to have?"

"Oh, I don't know, $175,000."

"OK, you got it."

That was it. Real simple. It took just a few minutes.

Herzog was getting tired of all the paperwork he had to do as general manager, so in 1982 he brought in Joe McDonald to take on some of the responsibilities as general manager. Whitey still made most of the personnel decisions, but McDonald was the guy who did the paperwork and negotiated contracts.

It was getting toward the end of the 1982 season. We hadn't won the division yet, but we were on our way to winning it, so I went to Whitey like I always did and said, "What about next year?"

"Yeah, I told Joe I want you back next year."

I went upstairs to see McDonald. "I just want to talk about next year," I said. "Whitey said he wants me back and he told me to come up and get a contract settled."

But McDonald started hemming and hawing. "Well, Andy Hassler is out there," he said. "And some other left-handers. I'm thinking about inviting you to spring training as a nonroster player." And I'm thinking, "What's going on here?"

I went down to see Whitey. "McDonald's giving me a different story," I said.

Time passed and we won the division and the National League pennant, and we went to the World Series and won the World Series, too. The season ended and I went home without a contract for 1983. During the winter, I was waiting to get a contract and McDonald finally acknowledged that I was going to be a roster player. He sent me a contract for the same money as the year before, $200,000.

I did some research and then I wrote a letter and sent it to McDonald pointing out that the average salary for a relief pitcher with at least six years of major league service was $435,000. I had 24

A Ring to It

I was sitting in front of my television set, sipping a glass of wine and watching the 1997 American League Championship Series between Baltimore and Cleveland, when they flashed a trivia question. Cal Ripken Jr. had gone 14 years since he played in the World Series. "What player has the greatest length of time between World Series appearances?"

I turned to my wife, Mary Ann, and said, "I think I'm the answer to that trivia question."

The next inning, they gave the answer. I was right. "Jim Kaat went 17 years between World Series appearances, from 1965 with Minnesota to 1982 with St. Louis."

That's why of all the years I spent in baseball, the 1982 season with the Cardinals was my greatest thrill in baseball. I wear that 1982 World Series ring proudly. It's the only one I ever got.

My name came up again when Ray Bourque was a member of the Stanley Cup–champion Colorado Avalanche in 2001. They made a big thing of the fact that Bourque finally won a championship in his 21st year in the NHL. I got a call from the Elias Sports Bureau informing me that I waited longer than Bourque to win a championship. When I was with the Cardinals in 1982 and we won the World Series, I was in my 24th major league season.

Of course, not many get to play that long. Nolan Ryan, for example, played two years longer than I did. But he played in the World Series with the Mets in 1969, in his third major league season. Nolie pitched for 24 more years and never got to the World Series again.

years of service and I was making $200,000. I wrote that I understood I wasn't going to go from $200,000 to $435,000, but I thought that after contributing to a team that won the World Series, $275,000 was a fair figure.

McDonald evidently went to Whitey and said that I was asking for $435,000 because I got a letter from Herzog scolding me. He said I was pricing myself out of the market. I tracked Herzog down by telephone and told him, "Whitey, that's not true. I told Joe McDonald what the average was and I told him exactly what I was asking."

That winter, the St. Louis baseball writers invited me to their annual dinner and I accepted. Just about that time, my dad's health took a turn for the worse—he eventually passed away on January 19—but he was in a coma for a week before he died, so I called the Cardinals and told them I wasn't going to be able to make the dinner because I was in Michigan with my dad. Whitey thought I skipped the writers' dinner out of defiance because of the contract thing and that strained my relationship with Whitey a little.

We got the contract settled. I signed for the $275,000 I was asking, and I reported to spring training for the 1983 season. That winter, the Cardinals had signed a minor league free agent named Dave Von Ohlen, a left-handed pitcher. The season started and Von Ohlen was on the team, and the phone would ring in the bullpen, and where it had always been my call, all of a sudden, it was Von Ohlen's. I said to our bullpen coach, Dave Ricketts, that I could tell they were phasing me out.

I didn't pitch much in the first half of the season. It got close to the All-Star break and we had a couple of pitchers hurt. In the last game before the All-Star break, I was brought in to pitch the last three innings and clean up in a lopsided win. After that, I told Bruce Sutter, "I think I'm going to get to start some games in the second half. We're playing San Francisco and San Diego. They've got a lot of left-handed hitters and we've got some guys that are hurt."

When I got home the next day, the phone rang and it was Joe McDonald. He said, "We just got a chance to pick up Dave Rucker from Detroit, this left-hander we've had our eyes on for a while. We're releasing you."

"You're what?"

"Yeah," he said. "We're releasing you. We're going to go with the younger guy."

Going with a younger guy? Come on, Joe, I still hadn't reached my 45th birthday.

Radio Daze

My baseball odyssey begins in the unlikely town of Zeeland, Michigan, situated in the westernmost part of the state, about 150 miles west of Detroit and 120 miles north of Chicago—in other words, far from the nearest major league city.

I was the youngest of four children of John and Nancy Kaat, an unplanned arrival. Mom and Dad were both in their late thirties when I came along. My sisters, Mildred and Esther, and my brother, Bill, from nine to thirteen years older than I, all married relatively young, so I grew up almost as an only child.

Zeeland was a Dutch enclave whose primary industries were chicken and turkey hatching and furniture making. In the area where I grew up, a lot of the towns are named after Dutch towns, such as Holland, Drenthe, Beaver Dam, and Zeeland. Dad worked in the local hatchery, and Mom was a homemaker. They were both born in this country, but their ancestors came here from the Netherlands.

The name Kaat is Dutch and is pronounced "Cot," but early in my career most people pronounced my name "Cat," and I never bothered to correct them. In fact, one year they misspelled my name on my bubble gum card and it came out "Katt."

For obvious reasons, when I began playing professional baseball, I picked up the nickname "Kitty." It started in the spring of 1958 with a left-handed pitcher named Chuck Stobbs. At the time, Chuck was an 11-year veteran who had won 89 major league games but who was best known, unfortunately, for serving up the pitch in 1953 that Mickey Mantle hit clear out of Washington's Griffith Stadium. It became famous as Mantle's "tape-measure" home run that the Yankees' public relations director, Red Patterson, supposedly measured at 565 feet. I say "supposedly" because Mantle, himself, years later said he believed Patterson never left the press box. Whatever the distance, it was one of the longest home runs in baseball history, and it served to help create the legend of Mickey Mantle.

In my first spring training, everybody called me "Cat." Stobbs used to kid me about having a brother "Bob" and another brother, "Tom." There were three crusty veterans in camp—Stobbs, Russ Kemmerer, and Truman Clevenger—and when they saw me on the mound in fielding drills, I reminded them of Harry the "Cat" Brecheen and Harvey Haddix, the "Kitten," who were quick off the mound and good fielders. They started calling me the "Kitten." Because I was the youngest pitcher in camp, I became the "little Kitty Cat," and that's how that all evolved, and it's stayed with me to this day.

I once asked Mom what the word *Kaat* means in Dutch, and the closest she could come to a definition was "tennis."

It was my dad who nurtured my love for baseball. John Kaat never played the game professionally, but he was known in our area as "Mr. Baseball." He was the source for any baseball information, including scoring and umpiring disputes in the local softball leagues. Fast-pitch softball was the only organized ball in our town. Little League had not yet reached our corner of the world, and American Legion ball was for older kids, so softball was the popular game.

In the evenings, when dad came home from work, we played baseball trivia or talked baseball. Dad was so knowledgeable about baseball, some people in town urged him to try to be a contestant on the *$64,000 Question*, a popular television show in the fifties, but he never pursued it. He just loved the game for the game. He passed that love of baseball on to me, and I took to it like Gaylord Perry to a jar of Vaseline.

Because of the distance, I rarely got to see a major league game. I saw my first one in Detroit in 1946. It was a Wednesday afternoon doubleheader, the Tigers and Red Sox. I was only seven, but I remember a lot about it. Hank Greenberg hit two home runs. Ted Williams hit two. Hal Newhouser pitched the first game for the Tigers and hit a home run. Newhouser beat Joe Dobson in the first game. The Red Sox won the second game. Boo Ferriss beat Dizzy Trout. The scores were 16–3 and 9–4, and they played each game in about two hours and 10 minutes. There were 46,000 people in the stands.

Mostly, I got my baseball on radio. We were fortunate to be located in such a position that we were able to pick up Chicago and Detroit radio stations, so I could always get a game. Sundays were the best days. There were always doubleheaders on Sundays. After church and one of Mom's great dinners, I'd settle down and listen to Bob Elson, the "Commander," describe White Sox games, or Harry Heilmann calling Tigers games, or Jack Brickhouse and Bert Wilson

11

on Cubs games. Later, when the Braves moved to Milwaukee, I'd pick up Earl Gillespie doing Braves games.

I collected baseball cards, read *The Sporting News*, checked the box scores of the major league games every day in the local newspaper, and had my radio. I was saturated with baseball and I loved it. And there was Dad. He loved baseball like no other person I've ever met. Connie Mack was his idol, his favorite team was the Philadelphia Athletics, and his favorite player was the great Robert Moses "Lefty" Grove, who had won 300 major league games in a 17-year career. Dad even drove to Cooperstown in 1947 for Grove's induction into the Hall of Fame, stopping on the way to visit Lefty's bowling alley in Lonaconing, Maryland. I regret to this day that I didn't make the trip to Cooperstown. I was only eight at the time.

It figured that I would also choose the Philadelphia Athletics as my favorite team. Psychologists might say it was my way of bonding with my dad, whom I admired, respected, and loved very much. If Dad's favorite player was a left-handed pitcher, mine would be, too. I chose Bobby Shantz, who won 24 games for the Athletics and was named the American League's Most Valuable Player (there was no Cy Young Award back then) in 1952.

One reason I was drawn to Shantz is that he was only 5'6", and as a youngster I was small for my age. They used to call me "Little Jimmy." When I was a junior in high school, I stood only 5'8" with no indication I would grow to my present height of 6'5". Bobby Shantz was my inspiration. I figured if he could make it to the major leagues at 5'6", I had a chance.

I developed my pitching motion by imitating Bobby. I saw pictures of him in *Sport Magazine*, cut them out, and taped them to my bedroom wall so I could study his motion. If there was a game on the radio and Shantz was pitching, I would listen intently as the announcers described his delivery—finishing square to the plate on the balls of his feet and taking a small hop toward home after delivering the pitch so as to be in perfect position to field a ball hit back to the mound. The next day, I would be outside, pitching rubber balls off the back of our garage at 44 Wall Street, trying to finish in the same position as Bobby Shantz.

Shantz was probably the greatest fielding pitcher of all time, quick as a cat and always on balance when he finished his delivery. He was adept at getting to bunts and making plays that most pitchers couldn't make.

They didn't begin awarding the Gold Glove for fielding until 1957. By then, Shantz was already in his ninth major league season. That first year, they awarded one Gold Glove at each position. Shantz, who was with the Yankees at the time, won it for pitchers. The following year, they awarded one Gold Glove at each position in each league. Shantz won it again. He won in 1959 and in 1960 with the Yankees. Bobby went to the National League in 1961 and won the Gold Glove with the Pirates. He won it with the Cardinals in 1962 and 1963, and with the Phillies in 1964, his last season in the major leagues.

Frank Lary of the Tigers won the Gold Glove for pitchers in the American League in 1961, the year Bobby left. I won it in 1962, and that began a streak in which I won 16 consecutive Gold Gloves, 14 in the American League, 2 in the National League, a record I proudly share with my friend, Hall of Famer Brooks Robinson. Bobby Shantz won the Gold Glove eight consecutive years, and I have no doubt that if he had remained in the American League, he would have won a few that I got, and that if they had been awarding the Gold Glove prior to 1957, Bobby would have had six or seven more.

In 1960, when I was playing for the Washington Senators, we were at Yankee Stadium for Old Timers' Day, and I had a picture taken with Lefty Grove and Bobby Shantz, my dad's favorite player and mine.

Years later, I was doing a Sunday night radio show for station KFAN in Minneapolis. I would telephone former players and talk to them. I tracked Shantz down at his home outside Philadelphia and had him as a guest on the show, and I told him I had patterned my pitching motion after his. He was pleased and said he was flattered, but Bobby is such a humble guy, he didn't make a big deal out of it.

Looking back a half century later, I realize I had an ideal childhood. I believe the stability of my home life, the strong work ethic I inherited from my dad, and the support I got from my parents and siblings had as much to do with my success as a major league pitcher as did my ability to throw strikes. There never was any jealousy of the attention I received, and they all went out of their way to attend my games, encourage me, enjoy my career, and share in my accomplishments.

Summers were the best of times. Each day, I would wake up early, grab my glove, and go to Berghorst's Gas Station where I met up with my neighborhood pals, Jim Wyngarden, Tom Bos, Jack Faber, Cal Burns, and the Raterink brothers, Jason and Junior, and we'd head for the local athletic field. I had a glove that was given to me by a real big leaguer, Frank "Stubby" Overmire, who pitched for the Tigers, the St. Louis Browns, and the Yankees in the forties and early fifties. He was a friend of my uncle John Boelema from Grand Rapids. Uncle John told Stubby how much I loved baseball and arranged for me to meet my first big-league ballplayer.

Stubby was a little guy, about 5'7" and left-handed like me. Meeting a real big leaguer was one of the early thrills of my life, and when he gave me one of his gloves, I was beside myself with joy.

Later, Stubby became a minor league manager with the Tigers, and when my career started, we crossed paths a lot in the Florida Instructional League. I had the chance to remind him that I got my first glove from him back in Grand Rapids, Michigan.

I was the only lefty in my crowd, and because we had only three or four players on a side in our summer games, not enough to cover the entire field, we had a rule that any ball hit to the right side of second base was an out. I had to learn to hit to left field, which taught me to wait on the ball and helped me become a pretty decent hitter for a pitcher when I reached the major leagues. We'd play a few hours in the hot summer sun, then return to Berghorst's for a Nehi soda pop and a bag of peanuts. We discovered that pouring the peanuts into pop was an extra tasty treat. Then it was back to the field to play again until it was dinnertime.

This was our daily summer routine. When it rained, we played "dice baseball." If you rolled 1-1, it was a single; 2-2 was a double; and so on. Every combination of numbers had a corresponding play. We used our Bowman bubble gum cards to make out our lineups and kept box scores of these games.

By following the local fast-pitch softball games, I became fascinated with how the pitcher could dominate. Lum Veldman was a local hero who racked up a lot of no-hitters and strikeouts, and I heard Dad talk constantly about Lefty Grove. I decided that's the position I wanted to play. It was obvious to me that the pitcher was the most important player on the field, the only one who was involved in every play. Nothing happened until he released the ball. If I had been born 25 years later, it might have been different. Through the years, the baseball hierarchy made it increasingly difficult for a pitcher to ply his trade by shrinking the strike zone, making the ball harder and livelier, and building the new parks "homer friendly."

The first organized baseball I played was American Legion. Holland, Michigan, about five miles from Zeeland, was the site of the summer American Legion league in our area. I tried out for a team sponsored by Padnos Scrap Iron and got my first pitching lesson from Ned Stuits, a coach at the local high school. He showed me how to stand on the pitching rubber, pivot, and step toward home. It was the only fundamental pitching instruction I ever had. The rest came from listening to the radio and mimicking the pictures of Bobby Shantz.

Because I wasn't big and didn't throw very hard, I developed other ways to get hitters out. I experimented, and perfected, a variety of curveballs, what in those days we called in-shoots, roundhouses, and drops. I made the Padnos Scrap Iron team and was their best pitcher. One of my fondest memories was the lead story in the *Holland Sentinel* that said, "Little Jimmy Kaat led the Legion All-Stars to victory over the Grand Rapids All-Stars by pitching a complete game and driving in the winning run with a home run in the eighth inning." Life couldn't get any better than that.

While I was playing Legion ball, I also served as batboy for our town team, the Chix, of the Southwestern Michigan Baseball League, which was made up of former high school and college players, some of whom even had a shot at pro ball. I looked up to guys like Ken Wiersma, the catcher, Howie De Jonge, the shortstop, Ted Boeve, an outfielder, and Junior De Jonge and Del Komejan, pitchers. I wanted to be as good as they were. The manager of the Chix, Marinus Scheele, was tough and profane—Earl Weaver before his time. After I had played one season of Legion ball, Scheele asked me if I wanted to pitch for the town team. I was only 17 and the players in the league were men in their twenties

16

and thirties, men with families, some with professional experience. I asked my dad for advice.

"You've proven you can pitch against American Legion hitters," Dad said. "Why not give it a shot?"

I was by far the youngest player in the league. When we played road games in surrounding towns I'd ride with the older guys. After the game, the team would stop at a watering hole on the way home. Everybody piled out of the cars and went in for a couple of beers, but you had to be 18 to enter one of those places, so I would remain in the car daydreaming about someday pitching in the major leagues. Every once in a while, one of the players, or our business manager/traveling secretary Ned Bergsma, would come out and bring me a soda pop and check to see if I was OK.

I had a terrific season for the Chix. I pitched well, hit well, and helped them win the league championship. At the same time, I also pitched for the Zeeland High School team, also called the Chix. I was getting my fill of baseball and loving every minute of it.

When I tried out for the high school team as a freshman, I was so small they cut my sweatshirt sleeves in half and they still covered my wrists. My high school coach, Bob Hoover, was a source of encouragement for me. When I was a junior, he asked the Detroit Tigers to invite me to a tryout camp they were holding in our area, but the Tigers said they weren't interested in pitchers who were only 5'8".

I had a successful high school career in both baseball and basketball and began to think about where I would go to college. None of my siblings had gone to college because my parents couldn't afford the tuition. I was hoping to get an athletic scholarship from Western Michigan in Kalamazoo. I had gained a measure of recognition in southwestern Michigan as a basketball player, but I wasn't a big enough star to merit a scholarship from a school like Western Michigan. I resigned myself to the thought that my best bet for a college education was at Hope College, a liberal arts school affiliated with the Reformed Church of America, a predominantly Dutch institution.

There was no scholarship from Hope. The best it could offer was arranging a summer job to help with my tuition. I had no other option, so I took a job working for the Borgman brothers at Model Laundry. I lifted heavy canvas bags of soiled linens and towels from the area motels and resorts and played baseball several nights a week. All that activity must have improved my appetite. When I graduated from high school, I stood 5'10". When I entered college a few months later, I was 6'3". Fortunately Mom was a seamstress. She kept altering my clothes or making me new ones.

I enrolled in Hope College in September of 1956, played freshman basketball, and looked forward to playing college baseball. Hope was a member of the Michigan Intercollegiate Athletic Association and a perennial power in the MIAA, a league that included Kalamazoo, Derek Jeter's hometown, and Alma, where former Detroit Tigers outfielder Jim Northrup went to school.

One day, I was pitching at Kalamazoo, and during warm-ups between innings, one got away from me. It hit the backstop with a resounding CRACK! Sitting in the stands was a Washington Senators area scout named Dick Wiencek, who later told me he had started dozing when the crack of the ball hitting the backstop awoke him with a start. It must have been fate. If not for that wild pitch, Wiencek might have slept through my start. But the crack caught his attention and I pitched a pretty good game, which impressed Dick enough that he showed up for my next start, a week later against Alma. I had another good game. It turned out that also in attendance were Morrie De Loof, a scout for the Red Sox, and Pete Milito, a well-known area scout for the White Sox.

I pitched six games in my freshman year, won all six, gave up just one earned run all year, and averaged better than a strikeout an inning and a walk a game. That was considered exceptional control for a left-hander. For some unexplained reason, left-handers always were thought to be erratic. I don't know why that is because pitchers such as Whitey Ford, Tommy John, and Tom Glavine, all left-handers, had excellent control.

In any case, a week after our college season ended, Wiencek asked if I would be interested in going to Chicago to work out for the Senators. Would I be interested? I could hardly control my excitement as Dad drove me to Chicago. I kept thinking about putting on a big-league uniform and standing on the same field with my bubble gum cards, Roy Sievers and Jim Lemon of the Senators, Nellie Fox and Chico Carrasquel of the White Sox.

I arrived in Comiskey Park and was taken to the visitors clubhouse where I was given a gray flannel Senators uniform with navy blue and red trim and a blue cap with a red *W*. Then I was taken onto the field and introduced to Harry "Cookie" Lavagetto, the Senators manager. Here my baseball education came in handy. I knew all about Lavagetto. I think I impressed Cookie when I told him I had listened to the 1947 World Series between the Yankees and Dodgers and had heard the famous fourth game from Ebbets Field in Brooklyn.

The Yankees starting pitcher, Bill Bevens, was one out away from pitching the first no-hitter in World Series history when Lavagetto hit a two-run, pinch-hit double off the wall in right field to score two runs and give the Dodgers a 3–2 victory.

I went to the mound and threw for about 15 to 20 minutes to veteran catcher Ed Fitz Gerald while Lavagetto and his pitching coach, Walter "Boom-Boom" Beck, watched. Strangely, although I was excited about being there, I wasn't nervous at all. My dad had calmed me on the ride from Zeeland by reminding me it was just a tryout. I threw all my pitches—a fastball and my variety of curveballs. I must have impressed Lavagetto because when I was finished throwing, Cookie said, "Kid, if you sign with us, you'll be in our starting rotation in three years."

Hearing that got my heart racing and my hopes up. I began to believe that my dream of being a big-league pitcher was not so far-fetched after all.

I showered and dressed, and then Dad and I watched the game from seats provided by the Senators. I was so excited and my mind was racing so rapidly, I don't remember much about the game except that the White Sox won.

On the ride home, I mentioned to Dad what Lavagetto said about me being in the Senators starting rotation in three years. Dad, with just the right amount of caution to keep my head from swelling, said, "Well, Jim, bear in mind he might say that to a lot of young men to encourage them to sign with his team."

Dad's words brought me gently down to earth, and my thoughts turned to what I was going to do that summer to earn money for my tuition. It was a decision I wouldn't have to make.

CHAPTER **3**

"Little Jimmy" Grows Up . . . and Turns Pro

The day after we returned from the tryout with the Senators in Chicago, I received a call from Dick Wiencek. He said the Senators were prepared to offer me a $4,000 signing bonus and send me to Superior, Nebraska, in the all-rookie Nebraska State League in two weeks. I was bowled over by the thought of being paid to play baseball, a summer job doing what I loved best. And the $4,000 bonus was nice, too.

Before long Pete Milito, the White Sox scout, called, and said he had heard I might sign to play pro ball. Apparently, there are no secrets among baseball scouts. It seemed that Pete, and several other scouts, had the impression I wouldn't sign because professional baseball was played on Sunday. I came from a strict Dutch community, and the general belief was that any activity on the Sabbath other than attending church was frowned upon. The great Christy Mathewson, who pitched for the New York Giants at the turn of the 20th century and won 373 games in 17 years, is the only player I heard of who was excused from playing ball on Sunday.

What the scouts didn't know was that my parents had no problem with me playing on Sunday. The philosophy taught to my siblings and me was that Sunday was a day to attend church and honor the Sabbath, but it was more important to live a consistent, respectful, responsible life seven days a week, not just one.

Dad liked to use the terms *consistency* and *moderation*. Christianity is based on faith and grace, not a rule book of do's and don'ts. I'm grateful my eternal destiny is not determined by how good or bad a person I am.

Having established that playing professional baseball caused me no moral dilemma, Milito said the White Sox were offering a $25,000 signing bonus.

I wasn't affected one bit by the large bonus offer. I had no concept of money. I couldn't tell you what Ted Williams was making, or Mickey Mantle, or Bobby Shantz, or any other player. I just knew I wanted to pitch in the big leagues. It was Dad, in his infinite wisdom, who helped me make the right decision.

At the time, there was a rule in major league baseball that any player receiving a signing bonus of more than $4,000 was required to spend his first two years on the major league roster. The purpose was to discourage the richer teams from cornering the market on the best young talent. If they had to carry these so-called bonus babies for two seasons, it would hurt those teams' chances of winning.

Dad followed the careers of these bonus babies and pointed out that players like Paul Pettit with the Pirates, Frank Baumann with the Red Sox, and Jim Small and "Diamond" Jim Brady with the Tigers never realized their full potential because they were forced to spend their first two years in the major leagues instead of learning their trade in the minor leagues. Even Sandy Koufax almost had his fabulous career stalled because he spent his first two years of professional ball with the Dodgers, riding the pines.

On the other hand, Jim Bunning didn't get a big bonus, but he went to the minor leagues, perfected his craft, worked his way up to the major leagues, and became a Hall of Fame pitcher.

Dad's advice was to decline the White Sox offer of $25,000 and take Washington's $4,000, go to the minor leagues, learn how to pitch, and work my way up to the majors. It had to be a great temptation for him to advise me to take the better offer. I can remember that every week when Dad brought home his paycheck, Mom would take it to the local gas station and get it cashed, $72 a week. The $25,000 the White Sox were offering represented almost seven years' pay for him, yet Dad had the wisdom and foresight to turn down the big money up front and take the lesser amount, sign with a team that was thin in left-handed pitching, go to the minor leagues, and learn the art of pitching.

Was it the right decision? You be the judge. When my career ended, I was 44 years old and I had played in the major leagues longer than any player in history, including Babe Ruth, Ty Cobb, Walter Johnson, and, in my opinion the greatest player ever and my all-time favorite, Hank Aaron.

Several years ago, a young pitcher from Texas named Todd Van Poppel was being touted as the next Nolan Ryan. His agent, Scott Boras, got him a lucrative, multimillion-dollar deal that included a guarantee he would be on the major league roster in a year or two. In that way, Van Poppel would get the mandatory major league minimum salary, service time in the lucrative Major League Players

Benefit Plan, and licensing revenue that is shared by all major leaguers. These are sound business decisions, and I have great respect for
Boras as a person and an agent who gets top dollar for his clients.

After all, that's his job.

However, from a career standpoint, I'm sure Van Poppel, and
many others like him, never realized their full potential because they
didn't have the benefit of learning in the minor leagues. Van Poppel
never became the pitcher everyone thought he would be, and I'm
convinced he would have been better served, and the money he got
on the front end would be peanuts compared to what he might have
made, if he had John Kaat advising him instead of Scott Boras.

My decision made, I signed a contract on June 17, 1957. John
and Nancy Kaat's son, "Little Jimmy," was a professional baseball
player. The "Little Jimmy" tag would disappear quickly. I was now
6'3" and 185 pounds. And I eagerly awaited the day when I would
leave for Superior, Nebraska.

My travel instructions came from the Washington Senators
minor league office along with a plane ticket from Grand Rapids to
Omaha, by way of Minneapolis. In Omaha, I would catch a bus to
Superior. The plan was for Mom to take me to the airport at about
noon. Dad went to work, as usual, and would come home during his
lunch hour to see me off, which he did. In so doing, he caused me to
experience something I had never seen in my 18 years. While he was
saying good-bye, John Kaat, as tough as they come, broke down and
cried. I had never seen an emotional side of him, except the emotion
he showed when he was doling out discipline.

It suddenly was clear to me that Dad loved baseball so much, followed it so closely, and studied it so intently, he was overcome by the
idea that his son was going off to play the game as a professional.
These were tears of joy. In spite of myself, I started crying, too. I

remember the scene as if it were yesterday: the two of us standing on the steps just inside the back door of our home, arms wrapped around each other, the tears flowing freely. It's one of the fondest memories of my life.

I arrived in Superior in the late afternoon and found the hotel that served as the team's headquarters. It was the only hotel in town. I noticed a lot of other young men and figured they were my teammates. At our first team meeting the next day, I met guys from New York, California, North Carolina, Georgia. Suddenly, a flood of thoughts came to my mind. Did they play the game differently from how I played? Was I in over my head? Was I going to be able to compete at this level?

Up to that point, I had competed only against players from my home area, never on a national or interstate level. I was suddenly afflicted with self-doubt.

Our manager was Ray Baker, the brother of Floyd Baker, who had been a big-league infielder for 13 seasons with five teams and who would be our third-base coach a few years later when I was with the Twins. Floyd was soft-spoken, encouraging, and helpful. His brother, Ray, was Floyd's antithesis—short on patience, profane, and sour. If we were having a bad game, he would leave our dugout and sit on a bench down the foul line as if disavowing any connection with us.

In Superior, I shared an upstairs apartment with another pitcher, Roger Herr from York, Pennsylvania, in the home of a widow who was very maternal toward us. We got the room and she did our laundry and frequently cooked us breakfast, all for $16 a week. I was living comfortably, enjoying life, and beginning to spread my wings.

I was in the local drugstore one evening when I spotted one of the prettiest girls I had ever seen. She was a California blonde, the kind you see on the cover of a surfing magazine. She was from Camarillo and was in Superior visiting her grandmother. I got up the courage to introduce myself and invited her to a movie and a stroll through the park. When it was time for her to return home to California, we exchanged addresses and the promise to stay in touch. In about a week, I received a nice letter on perfumed stationery. In her letter, she explained that she had bought a couple of boxes of stationery so she could write me regularly.

Needless to say, I was feeling pretty good about myself, until a few days later when I spotted the same stationery on the chair of one of my teammates, a New Yorker named Ray White. I had developed a good relationship with Ray, a cocky guy with a swagger, but very likable. I asked Ray about the stationery, and it turned out that the same honey blonde who was writing to me also was writing to him, on the same perfumed stationery. We both wondered how many other players on the team were getting letters on that same stationery. Welcome to the world of professional sports!

If you asked today's millionaire ballplayers about their experience in the minor leagues, I'm sure most of them would tell you how much fun they had. When you're in the minors, you don't know how pampered a major leaguer is because you haven't been there. You don't miss what you don't know. I had a ball in my years in the minors.

I remember the long bus rides, the midnight stops at all-night diners, being entertained by one of your teammates who happens to be a guitar player and singer. Charlie Pride, the country-and-western singer, got his start when he was a minor league player in Pocatello, Idaho, and would entertain his teammates on long bus rides.

A highlight of our Nebraska trips was counting the jackrabbits, as big as kangaroos, running across the highway in front of our bus. Mosquitoes in Holdredge were the biggest I've ever seen. In North

Platte, I got a thrill meeting their manager, Rudy York, a slugging first baseman for the Tigers and Red Sox in the thirties and forties. I had a lot of Rudy York baseball cards when I was a kid.

In Kearney, I pitched against the Yankees farm team managed by Randy Gumpert, a former major league pitcher. I went the distance and struck out 12, most of them with a good twelve-o'clock-to-six-o'clock curveball I called a drop.

When the season ended and we took our last bus ride home after playing the Grand Island Athletics, our manager, Ray Baker, went up and down the aisle of the bus critiquing each player. When he came to me, he said, "Kid, if you come up with a good enough fastball, you have a chance to go places."

I was buoyed by these words of praise from a manager who didn't give compliments easily. My season was just mediocre. I won 5 and lost 6, with an ERA of 3.70, but I was not discouraged. It was a big adjustment living away from home for the first time and learning to be a baseball player every day, not just a few nights a week.

When I returned to Zeeland after the season, Dad asked me to assess my performance. I said I found out that I could compete on that level and I was ready for the next step.

I went back to Hope College for the fall semester, but I couldn't keep my mind on my studies. I kept thinking about spring training. Dick Wiencek had arranged for me to go to the major league camp and I couldn't wait. The time passed slowly during the fall and winter. I kept counting the days until spring training, like a kid waiting for Christmas. I thought the day would never come when I would leave for Orlando, Florida.

Dreams Coming True

"**H**ey, kid, you look like Bobby Shantz fielding those ground balls." The booming voice of Washington Senators pitching coach Walter "Boom-Boom" Beck resounded throughout old Tinker Field and took me by surprise. How did he know that Shantz was my favorite player when I was a kid and that I copied his pitching motion and follow-through?

I had been in the Senators training camp, my first training camp, only a few days. I was 19 years old, and the extent of my professional experience was two months in a rookie league. I knew I had no chance to make the team. I had no illusions about that. I was there because Dick Wiencek, the scout who signed me, had arranged for me to go to spring training with the Senators as a nonroster invitee, and I had been looking forward eagerly to the experience.

The winter had passed slowly as I waited anxiously for the day when I would report to spring training. I had received my contract in January. I would make a whopping $350 a month and was

29

assigned to the Fox Cities Foxes in the Class B Three-I League, so called because it was made up of teams from Illinois, Indiana, and Iowa. But Fox Cities was in Appleton, Wisconsin. So what was it doing in the Three-I League?

Originally, the team was in Peoria, Illinois, but declining attendance—a common problem in the minor leagues in those days—caused the Senators to move the team to Fox Cities. Fox Cities was managed by Pete Suder. That was a name I knew because he had been a second baseman for the Philadelphia Athletics, my favorite team, and I was looking forward to playing for him.

A few days after I received my contract, I got my letter of invitation to report to the Washington Senators training camp in Orlando, Florida. Finally, the day arrived when I was scheduled to leave, and I could hardly contain my excitement as I boarded a DC3 from Grand Rapids to Orlando with several stops along the way. I landed at Herndon Airport in the late afternoon and took a cab to the Langford Hotel, the team's headquarters in Winter Park.

I would later learn that the Senators, and then the Minnesota Twins, was a tightfisted organization, but the team was staying in these posh digs because the executives were going to be there for six weeks and they wanted first-class treatment.

Winter Park, the home of Rollins College, was a lovely little upscale suburb about 15 miles from Orlando—which had a population of 35,000 at that time. This was before Disney World, of course.

Nonroster players dressed in a separate little building at rickety old Tinker Field. There wasn't enough room in the main clubhouse, which was a little wooden structure with a cold concrete floor and a wood-burning stove in the middle of the room. The training room was actually an area in the corner of the clubhouse where veteran Doc Lentz slapped on the analgesic balm and taped an ankle or two. I had met Doc when I tried out for the Senators at Comiskey Park the previous summer, and he treated me like I was one of the big leaguers. That was the start of a 16-year relationship with Doc.

I learned early that the proper way to use the training room was to stay away from it. It was a sign of weakness if you were always hanging around there. Get a little baby oil on your arm and back on cool mornings, then get out. If your arm got a little sore or tired, figure out a way to throw so it didn't bother you. I learned a lot that spring about pitching when your arm doesn't feel 100 percent.

Disabled list? It hardly existed back then. The lesson you learned early is that if you couldn't go to the post, someone else would take your place, and if he pitched well, you might not get your old job back. So, you learned to pitch with pain, or through it. In 25 years in the big leagues, once I got into the rotation, I never missed a start because of a tired arm or an arm injury. I was on the disabled list once, in July of 1972, when I broke my left wrist sliding into second base.

After we had dressed, we would wander over to the main clubhouse, and I was in awe at all the faces I recognized: Roy Sievers, Jim Lemon, Clint Courtney, Camilo Pascual, Pedro Ramos—my baseball card collection come to life.

My daily routine in spring training was to arrive early, which was no problem for me because when I was a boy, my dad worked as a milkman and I would often awaken at 5:00 A.M. and accompany him on his route. To this day, I'm still an early riser. By 7:30, I was already at Tinker Field, where I'd grab a cup of coffee, get in uniform, and sit around listening to our veteran coaches talk baseball.

There was Billy Jurges, who was an All-Star infielder for the Cubs and the Giants; Ellis Clary, one of the great storytellers; and pitching coach Walter "Boom-Boom" Beck, an old timer who had a career

31

record of 38–69 in 12 seasons with six teams: the St. Louis Browns, the Brooklyn Dodgers, the Philadelphia Phillies, the Detroit Tigers, the Cincinnati Reds, and the Pittsburgh Pirates. The story goes that he got his nickname when he won 12 games and lost 20 for the Dodgers in 1933 and had a penchant for giving up the long ball. A writer referred to him as "Boom-Boom" and, as so often happens in baseball, the name stuck with him for life.

When it was time to hit the field, we'd start out with calisthenics, then a game of catch to warm up your arm, and then we'd separate by position. For us pitchers, there was PFP, pitchers fielding practice, one of the rites of spring: covering first base on ground balls hit to the right side, getting off the mound quickly to field bunts, throwing to second base on a ground ball, and a few other fielding drills. Most pitchers viewed these drills as a boring, mundane routine. I attacked these sessions as if it was the seventh game of the World Series. I have always taken pride in my fielding and saw it as just another way to be successful as a pitcher.

It was while watching me in these drills that Chuck Stobbs pinned my nickname on me and Beck compared me with Bobby Shantz, the best compliment he could have given me.

I got to face Sievers, Lemon, Harmon Killebrew, and Bob Allison in intrasquad games, and I even got to pitch in an exhibition game. As a rookie pitcher, I went along on every bus trip we made in spring training. I was on those trips to sit in the bullpen and be ready in case the game went into extra innings and all the regular pitchers had been used. I was happy to be on those trips. It was an opportunity to see the other spring training ballparks and other major leaguers.

I got my chance to pitch in Clearwater, against the Phillies, the first major league team I ever faced. The game was tied in the eleventh inning and we were out of pitchers, so I was brought in. I gave up a single to Solly Hemus, hit Pancho Herrera with a pitch, walked Stan Lopata, and faced Willie "Puddin' Head" Jones with the bases loaded. That was a thrill for me. I must have had two dozen Puddin' Head Jones baseball cards. I didn't even feel bad when he singled off me to drive in the winning run.

After a few weeks, my time in the major league camp was coming to an end. Those of us not on the major league roster were sent to the minor league camp in Fernandina Beach, Florida, known to veteran minor leaguers as "Iwo Jima." It was windy and sandy, with bad fields and bad food. This wasn't sunny Florida with palm trees and pristine lakes. It was more like south Georgia.

One day, I was approached by a 28-year-old catcher named Jack McKeon—the same Jack McKeon who would manage in the major leagues with Kansas City, Oakland, San Diego, and Cincinnati and who would become known as "Trader Jack" when he was the general manager of the San Diego Padres. He was going to be the player/manager of the Class C Missoula Timberjacks.

Apparently, McKeon had seen me throw, liked what he saw, and figured I could help him win in Missoula.

"If you play for me, I'm a playing manager and I'm a catcher," Jack said. "I can teach you about pitching."

I listened to him, and what he said made sense, even though it meant I would be dropping down a notch and pitching for a Class C team instead of a Class B team. McKeon did a great sales job on me, convincing me that it would be in my best interest to pitch for a manager who also would be my catcher. I went to Joe Haynes, who was a Senators vice president and had something to do with the farm department, and asked him what he thought of the idea. He said it was fine with him, so when spring training ended, off I went to pitch for Jack McKeon in Missoula, Montana, in the Class C Pioneer League.

I started out the year 1–4, and some doubts about my ability began to creep into my mind. I had been in the rookie league the year before, and I thought, I can't go back to a rookie league, that's a one-time deal. Here I was supposed to be in Class B, and I was having trouble winning one notch below.

McKeon called me into his office and gave me a pep talk. He said, "You're going to be here all year; you're going to pitch every four days; the organization likes you." That relaxed me, and all of a sudden things started clicking and I turned my season around.

Joe Haynes and Sherry Robertson of the Senators front office came down to watch me pitch against Idaho Falls, and I pitched a good game. I struck out double figures and shut them out. But I still wasn't throwing very hard. I was young and growing, and my body was catching up. I had a good curve and a knack for pitching, but my fastball was not up to big-league standards. So Haynes and Robertson told McKeon they didn't think I was going to make it. Jack said, "I'll bet you a steak dinner he makes it."

I wound up leading the league in just about every category. After my slow start, I ended up 16–9, so I won 15 of my last 20 decisions, and that was in 125 games. With playoffs, I wound up pitching close to 250 innings. You'd pitch nine innings, and between starts you might come in to face a man or two in relief. That's unheard of today, but there were no pitch counts back then. I owe a lot to Jack McKeon. Going with him ended up being the right decision. I learned a lot about pitching from him, and he took a liking to me. He was always in my corner. Years later, when he was in Kansas City and he had Paul Splittorff, a left-hander I think reminded Jack of me, McKeon would often talk about me being one of his favorites.

The next year I moved up to Chattanooga in the Southern Association, a Class AA league. That's a big jump from Class C. There were a lot of veterans and former major leaguers in that league. The cities were bigger, and we traveled by train instead of by bus.

I was having just a so-so season. My highlight was setting the Southern Association record by striking out 19 in Nashville. In my next start, I struck out the first four batters, and all of a sudden I felt some soreness in my shoulder. Nowadays, they'd call it a rotator cuff. It was a career ender for a lot of pitchers. They didn't have MRIs in those days, or X rays, so my manager, Red Marion, brother of the great Cardinals shortstop Marty Marion, said, "Take 10 days off."

They didn't have rehab programs, so I went home to Michigan; while I was home, I listened on the radio to the game in which Harvey Haddix of the Pirates pitched 12 perfect innings against the Milwaukee Braves, then lost the game in the thirteenth. The date was May 26, 1959. When I returned to Chattanooga, I got back into the rotation, but I wasn't throwing the same. My arm didn't feel right, and I guess to compensate for the discomfort, I was dropping down a little. Wouldn't you know, Marion called me in and said, "You're going to the big leagues."

I was surprised. There had been talk that one of our pitchers was going to get called up, but I never thought it would be me. I was only 20 years old, I had pitched fewer than two seasons in the minor leagues, and I wasn't doing that well. We had other pitchers, Jack Kralick, Wade Wilson, and John Romanosky, all pitching better than I was.

When Red told me I was going up, I said, "My arm's still not 100 percent."

Red said, "You go up and let them take care of it up there."

I joined the Senators in Chicago on August 1. The first thing I did was go in to the manager's office to see Cookie Lavagetto. I reminded him that when I tried out for the Senators right there in Chicago, he told me if I signed with them, I'd be in the big leagues in three years.

"You were wrong, Cookie," I said. "I made it in two and a half years."

"Kid, You Don't Have a Chance"

joined the Senators in Chicago on a Saturday, and I was told I'd be starting the second game of a doubleheader the next day against the "Go-Go" White Sox—Luis Aparicio and Nellie Fox and that crowd, who would go on to win the American League pennant in 1959.

Unfortunately, my parents and my aunt and uncle had arrived in Chattanooga the day before I got called up. I got to spend some time with them, but they didn't see me pitch. They had driven from Michigan, and there wasn't enough time for them to make it back to Chicago to see my major league debut.

When I joined the Senators, they had lost something like 17 straight games. In old Comiskey Park, the visiting clubhouse was upstairs above the home dugout. During the first game of the Sunday doubleheader, I sat in the clubhouse, biding my time and waiting for my turn to pitch. Veteran Russ Kemmerer lost the first game of the doubleheader in a heartbreaker, 2–1. I was rubbing up the baseball getting ready to go down to warm up for game two, and the players filed into the clubhouse. Kemmerer looked at me and said, "Kid, you don't have a chance."

Walter Beck, our pitching coach, was furious with him. Kemmerer was just frustrated. He had pitched a great game, but we were losing every day. I got knocked out in the third inning of the second game, and they could tell that I wasn't throwing the same way I had in the spring. They asked me about it, and I told them there was something bothering me in my shoulder or my back. I had it checked out, and the doctor found that from pitching while the muscle was still healing, scar tissue had built up. I also had a cyst between my ribs. I had the cyst removed and they shut me down for six weeks. The next time I pitched was in September, against the Red Sox in Fenway Park. There I was, a 20-year-old kid facing the man many baseball people consider the greatest hitter who ever lived: Ted Williams.

I started one more game in 1959, and then the season was over. I had appeared in three games, had two starts, pitched seven innings, was 0–2, and had an earned run average over 12.

I went to spring training in 1960 with no guarantee I would make the team, but I had a pretty good spring and I was considered one of the Senators' top prospects. The team wasn't going anywhere. We had won only 63 games and finished last in 1959, so I figured because I could get some major league experience and they could get a good look at me, I might make the team, and I did.

I remember Opening Day of the 1960 season, the only time I ever was in Washington on Opening Day. President Eisenhower was there to throw out the first ball from the presidential box alongside our dugout. The protocol was for players from both teams to gather

"Kid, You Don't Have a Chance"

near first base. The president threw the ball up in the air. There was a big scrum, and Clyde McCullough, our bullpen coach, came up with the ball. It was a big thing to get that ball and then get the president to autograph it.

I started the second or third game of the season against the Red Sox, pitched well, and came out with a one-run lead in the eighth inning. The Red Sox came back and won the game, so I didn't get the win.

About a week later, on April 27, I started against Whitey Ford at Yankee Stadium. Moose Skowron hit a three-run home run off me. I gave up four runs

"Hello, Louis"

Chicago, August 2, 1959. I was making my first major league start against the "Go-Go" White Sox, so naturally I was excited. But it wasn't only because it was my first major league start.

I was warming up and Louis Armstrong was performing on a flatbed truck between games. I was a trumpet player when I was a kid, and I was a big Louie Armstrong fan, so I was warming up, thinking about pitching to Luis Aparicio and Nellie Fox, and I was also paying attention to Louis Armstrong going around entertaining the fans.

Oh, how I wish now I had the courage to go over and introduce myself to him.

in seven innings, but three of the runs were unearned. In the top of the eighth, Jim Lemon hit a three-run home run off Ford to put us up, 5–4. In those days, you didn't sit in the dugout or ice your arm when you were finished pitching. You just went in and took a shower because they didn't want you to stiffen up. I took my shower, and then I sneaked out and watched the rest of the game from the stands. Pedro Ramos pitched the last two innings and held them, and that was my first major league win—in Yankee Stadium, against Whitey Ford and the Yankees.

I was flattered when somebody told me that the legendary Yankees manager Casey Stengel was talking about me after the game and said, "That young feller throws harder than anybody since Herb Score."

They were talking about how many strikeouts I had in Class C at Missoula, and Stengel said, "I don't care if it's in the Epworth League, that's a lot of strikeouts."

The game at Yankee Stadium against Ford was the only game I won that season. I wasn't pitching well, but Cookie called me into his office and said, "We're not going anywhere, so you're going to pitch every four days." I started against Detroit and gave up back-to-back homers to Rocky Colavito and Chico Fernandez, and Cookie called me in after the game and said, "We changed our minds."

It was like one of those good news/bad news jokes. "The good news is you're going to pitch every four days. The bad news is you're going to do it in Charleston."

Charleston was our Triple A team. Going there was the best thing for me. It was obvious I wasn't ready for the big leagues. I pitched in 13 games for Washington that season, made nine starts, had a 1–5 record, and had an earned run average over 5.

Because I had missed so much time after my back surgery, that fall the Senators sent me to the Florida Instructional League in St. Petersburg so that I could get in more work and continue to improve. It was while I was in the Instructional League that we got word that the American League had approved the relocation of our team from Washington to Minnesota. One day we were the Washington Senators, and the next day we were the Minnesota Twins.

I remembered reading about how the Braves were treated in Milwaukee after they moved there from Boston in 1953. It was the same with us in Minnesota. We were treated like royalty. Automobile dealers furnished us with cars to use during the season; we got free meals at restaurants, all kinds of perks.

We weren't a very good team in 1961, our first year in Minnesota, but we led the league in attendance. I was in the regular rotation, and I stayed there all season. I won only 9 games and lost 17, but I was learning how to pitch. I made 29 starts, completed 8, and pitched my first shutout. My earned run average was a respectable 3.90.

Midway through the season, Cookie Lavagetto was fired as manager and replaced by Sam Mele. We finished seventh in what was now a 10-team American League. For the first time, the American League added expansion teams: the Washington Senators, which replaced our team that had moved to Minnesota, and the Los Angeles (later California, then Anaheim) Angels.

We were a young team made up of a lot of guys who had come through the farm system together. Our future was promising. We had pretty much cornered the market on players from Cuba, most of them scouted and signed by Papa Joe Cambria, who wasn't even Cuban (he actually was born in Italy), but he had a pipeline to Cuba and an eye for talent. Papa Joe signed more than four hundred players and was responsible for delivering Cubans Camilo Pascual, Carlos Paula, Bert Cueto, Julio Becquer, Sandy Valdespino, Jose Valdivielso, and, later, Zoilo Versalles and Tony Oliva to the Twins. He also delivered one of the great characters of my time, Pedro Ramos.

Pedro was a flamboyant, fun-loving guy who wore cowboy boots and a cowboy hat and always had a big Cuban cigar stuck in his mouth. His nickname was "Hots," short for hot dog, which is what you were called if you were a little cocky and liked to show off a bit. Pedro was more than a little cocky the way he strutted around with his cowboy hat and boots and that big cigar.

41

"I'm Facing Ted Williams"

Early in the 2002 season, the Yankees made their first trip of the season to Boston, and I was with them in my role as a television broadcaster. John Vander Wal was new to the Yankees and to the American League, in Fenway Park for the first time. John is from my part of the country, a Dutch fellow from Michigan. I spotted him coming out of the dugout and looking around.

"Your first trip to Fenway?" I said.

"Yeah."

"What do you think of it?"

"It's kind of old and small."

I remembered the first time I came to Fenway Park in September of 1959. We stayed at the Kenmore Hotel and I couldn't wait to walk out to Fenway. I got there early in the afternoon and there was Ted Williams playing pepper with Tom Yawkey, the owner of the Red Sox, and Johnny Orlando, the clubhouse man, which Ted did every day. I walked out to the left-field wall, the famous "Green Monster," and looked at all the dents in the wall, and I thought about Jimmie Foxx and Joe DiMaggio and Hank Greenberg, all the guys that put those dents in that wall.

That day, I got called out of the bullpen. It was the seventh inning and there I was, facing the great Ted Williams. I turned around to our second baseman, John Schaive, and I looked at him with my back to the plate and I mouthed, "I'm facing Ted Williams."

It was such a thrill; I couldn't wait to get back to the hotel and call home to tell my dad I pitched against Ted Williams.

I didn't do too well against him the first few times I faced him, but the next year, I started against the Red Sox and got Williams out. The following day, he and Pete Runnels were around the batting cage, and they were telling Roy Sievers and Jim Lemon how impressed they were with me.

I had met Ramos in my first spring training camp, and I took an immediate liking to him. He loved to compete, and he had a rubber arm. I liked playing catch with him. If he had thrown 20 minutes of batting practice the day before, he would cut it loose the next day when most pitchers wouldn't even pick up a ball.

Ramos used to boast that he could outrun anybody in baseball. He was always challenging Mickey Mantle to a race, but Mantle never would accept the challenge. How would it look if the great No. 7 was beaten in a footrace by a pitcher?

One day in spring training, Ellis Clary called his good friend George "Foghorn" Myatt, a coach for the Phillies, and said, "We've got a player who can outrun Ashburn."

Richie Ashburn was the Phillies Hall of Fame center fielder who would later become a broadcaster for the Phillies and one of the most beloved people in the game. In 1959, Ashburn was at the peak of his career, a leadoff hitter with great speed who made his living by slapping the ball around and running down fly balls in the outfield. Ellis' guy was "Hots," Pedro Ramos.

Myatt got some backers for Ashburn, and Clary got some for Ramos, and the match race was arranged on the day the Phillies came to Orlando for an exhibition game.

The Phillies bus arrived at 11:00 A.M. Both runners were given a few minutes to warm up, and the race was set. We gathered down the left-field line, which was the starting line. The finish line was where Clary was standing in center field. One of the coaches was the starter. He grabbed a towel, said, "Ready . . . set . . ." then dropped the towel and that was the signal for the runners to take off.

It was neck and neck for 60 yards with Ramos about a foot ahead of Ashburn when suddenly down went Richie. He had torn his hamstring and wound up missing the first few weeks of the season.

Manager Eddie Sawyer fined Ashburn, and that was the end of spring training match races.

The Twins were the first team that was an area franchise, the first to represent a state instead of a city. We played our games in Bloomington, which is midway between Minneapolis and St. Paul. Rather than slight one city or the other, and as a way of getting support from both cities, we weren't the St. Paul Saints or Minneapolis Millers but the Minnesota Twins. And the insignia on our caps was TC. We'd go around the league and people would ask what TC meant. They didn't realize it stood for Twin Cities. We'd always kid and say it stood for Twenty Cubans.

CHAPTER 6

Sandy K (as in Strikeout)

Things started to come together for the Twins in 1962, our second year in Minnesota. It was the year after Roger Maris hit 61 homers. Harmon Killebrew, who had hit 46 home runs the previous year, led the league with 48, 15 more than Maris and 18 more than Mickey Mantle. Harmon also led the league with 126 RBIs. Bob Allison was getting better. He hit 29 homers and drove in 102 runs. Zoilo Versalles was in his second year and becoming one of the better shortstops in the game. Rich Rollins came up from the minor leagues and took over at third base. Two years before, we had made a trade and got catcher Earl Battey and first baseman Don Mincher from the White Sox for Roy Sievers.

Camilo Pascual won 20 games, and I had a great year. I won 18 and led the league in shutouts with five. We hung with the Yankees almost to the end and wound up second, five games out of first.

Killebrew was becoming the premier home-run hitter in the American League and the offensive leader for the Twins. Harmon is a special person in a lot of ways, not only on the ball field. He was just about as classy a player as you'd want to play with. I never saw him throw his helmet or break a bat in anger. He was the epitome of a team leader, a superstar who led by example. In retrospect, we could have used a little more of a firebrand-type player on our ballclub. That just wasn't Harmon's style. He was always even keel, perfect for the upper Midwest. He was like Paul Bunyan. He hit these majestic, long home runs. And he wasn't a very big man, about 5'10", 195 pounds.

Killebrew never was a great defensive player. The Twins were always looking for a position for him. They tried him at third base, first base, and the outfield. Yet in Payette, Idaho, he had been a terrific high school quarterback who had a lot of offers to play football in college. And he came up as a second baseman—hard to picture Harmon Killebrew as a second baseman.

The only negative thing about Harmon is that he was so easygoing. Calvin Griffith, the owner of the Twins, would sign Killebrew easily every year. Harmon never made demands; he just took what was offered. Griffith knew that, so he would make sure to get Harmon signed early; then when the rabble-rousers like me would go in and try to get more money, Calvin would say, "Killebrew doesn't give me any trouble. I got him signed." Harmon made it a little more difficult for the rest of us because if the team leader was signed, it was hard for anybody else to hold out.

Sometimes you have to take a step back before you go forward, and that's what happened to us in 1963. We dropped back to third, even though Pascual won 21 games, Killebrew again led the league in homers with 45, and we got some help from a rookie outfielder named Jimmie Hall. I slipped to 10–10.

The next year, we fell all the way to sixth (tied with Cleveland), although Killebrew again led the league with 49 homers. Despite

Harmon Killebrew fell to 25 homers and 75 RBIs, but Zoilo Versalles was the MVP, although I thought Oliva should have won it. Tony batted .321 and won his second straight batting championship. He's still the only player in history to win batting titles in his first two years. He also drove in 98 runs. Don Mincher, Killebrew, Bob Allison, and Jimmie Hall each hit 20 home runs or more. Zoilo hit 19 and Oliva 16. Mudcat Grant won 21 games, and I won 18.

The Dodgers had won the National League pennant by two games over the Giants. They didn't have a regular who batted .300. Their RBI leader was Ron Fairly with 70. Lou Johnson and Jim Lefebvre tied for the team lead in home runs with 12. They hit only 78 home runs as a team, fewest in the major leagues by a wide margin, but they stole 172 bases, 94 of them by Maury Wills. And they had that great pitching staff. Sandy Koufax was 26–8 with a 2.04 ERA, 382 strikeouts in 336 innings, 27 complete games, and eight shutouts. Don Drysdale won 23 games, and Claude Osteen won 15.

The World Series opened in Minnesota. Mudcat Grant got the Game 1 assignment for us against Drysdale, who was pitching instead of Koufax because it was a Jewish holiday. I would draw Koufax in Game 2. Just my luck.

We knocked Drysdale out in the third inning when we scored six runs, including Versalles' three-run homer. We won, 8–2.

When it came out that Koufax would miss Game 1 because of Yom Kippur, my first thought was, "Wow, that's going to be pretty neat, facing Sandy Koufax."

I had never seen him pitch in person. In fact, the only time I had seen him pitch was on television in the 1963 World Series. There was only one *Game of the Week* in those days, on Saturday afternoon with Pee Wee Reese and Dizzy Dean, and when that was on we were playing, so I never saw the game. I never even saw Koufax pitch in spring training. I had heard about him, of course, but I had never seen him, so this was going to be my first look at him up close.

We were in the bullpen warming up for Game 2. It was a cold, damp, Minnesota autumn afternoon. The bullpens were right next to each other, and we were so close I could have reached out and touched him. I could hear his ball going "whoosh" while I was throwing my little "pffft . . ." He looked over at me and said, "You guys don't play in this weather, do you?" And I thought, "Maybe we've got a chance because we're used to playing in the cold and they're not."

The game started, and we both went three up, three down in the first few innings. I got them out in the third, and I came into the dugout and sat next to Johnny Sain, our pitching coach. "John," I said, "if I give up a run, this game's over. There's not a man alive can hit this guy. Where'd he come from?"

In the fifth, Bob Allison made one of the great catches in World Series history. If it had been in New York, they would have remembered it like Willie Mays' catch on Vic Wertz in the 1954 World Series. There was a man on, and Jim Lefebvre hit a screaming line drive into the left-field corner; Allison skidded in the mud and made a great catch to keep them from scoring.

In the sixth, we eked out a couple of runs off Koufax. There was an error by Jim Gilliam, a couple of scratch hits, and a double by Oliva, and we were ahead, 2–0. In the seventh, they got a couple of hits, and John Roseboro singled in a run to make it 2–1. With runners on second and third and one out, they took Koufax out for a pinch-hitter, Don Drysdale, which shows you what they thought of their bench. I struck out Drysdale and got Wills to pop to center to keep our lead at 2–1. Then we tacked on a run in the bottom of the seventh after Koufax was gone. In the eighth, the Dodgers walked

Frank Quilici in front of me, and I drove in two runs with a single off my future teammate and golf partner, Ron Perranoski. We won the game, 5–1, and were looking pretty good, leading the Series, two games to none.

From that point on, the Dodgers' pitching took control of the Series. Osteen shut us out in Game 3, Drysdale came back and beat us, 7–2, in Game 4, and Koufax pitched a four-hitter, struck out 10, and beat us, 7–0, in Game 5. I was knocked out in the third inning. Back in Minnesota, we won Game 6 when Mudcat Grant beat Osteen, 5–1. That meant that I would face Koufax again in Game 7, both of us pitching with only two days' rest.

We matched zeroes for three innings. The Dodgers had two hits and we had one. In the fourth, Lou Johnson led off with a home run. Ron Fairly doubled, Wes Parker singled, and that was it for me.

We had our one shot at Koufax in the fifth. Quilici doubled with one out, and Rich Rollins walked, which got Drysdale to start warming up in the bullpen. The Dodgers had just moved third baseman Jim Gilliam toward the foul line. Versalles hit a shot inside the bag that would have been a double and perhaps tied the game if Gilliam hadn't been moved. But he made a terrific backhanded stop and forced Quilici at third. After that, we didn't get a sniff of Koufax.

Because he was coming back after only two days' rest, Koufax didn't throw many curveballs. He tried to throw a few early in the game, but he wasn't getting them over, so he scrapped the curve and stuck with nothing but fastballs, one after another, and nobody could touch him. He was so overpowering, I actually felt sorry for our hitters. I batted four times against Koufax in the Series and it was a joke. He'd throw me that old "radio ball"—you can hear it, but you can't see it. The only time I put my bat on the ball was when I tried to bunt with two strikes and fouled it off. He was awesome.

51

Koufax went all the way, gave up only three hits, struck out 10, and beat us, 2–0. On two days' rest, no less. He ended the game, and the World Series, by striking out Earl Battey and Bob Allison with Killebrew on first base.

The next year, Koufax won 27 and lost 9, had a 1.73 earned run average, struck out 317 in 323 innings, and pitched 27 complete games and five shutouts. And then he retired because of an arthritic left elbow. He was only 31.

Talk about quitting on top. In his last four years, Koufax was 97–27 with ERAs of 1.88, 1.74, 2.04, and 1.73, and he had 89 complete games, 1,228 strikeouts, 31 shutouts, and three no-hitters, one of them a perfect game.

The year after he retired, Koufax worked for NBC on the *Game of the Week*. I'd see him from time to time when he did our games, and he always seemed uncomfortable. If we were on the *Game of the Week*, Sandy would come into our clubhouse and I'd see him looking around. There weren't a lot of guys in there he was familiar with, so he gravitated to me because we faced one another in the World Series and because we're both left-handed pitchers.

I see Sandy occasionally. He lives in Vero Beach, and I run into him at charity golf tournaments. When the Texas Rangers honored Nolan Ryan, he wanted Koufax there, and Sandy and I were staying at the same hotel. He was a friend of the Rangers' manager, Kevin Kennedy, from their Dodger days, and we sat around Kennedy's office and had a conversation. Later, I hooked up with him at the hotel. But that was the extent of it. I wouldn't say we're good friends. Sandy is not the kind of guy you can really get close to, but the times I've seen him, he's always cordial and always a gentleman. And he's still the best pitcher I've ever seen.

CHAPTER 7

Billy Brawl

You hear people say all the time that if you get to the World Series, you should make the most of the experience and enjoy it because you never know if you'll ever get there again. At the same time, when you do get to the World Series, you're so filled with success and a good feeling about your team, you believe you're going to have other chances to get there.

That's how I felt after we lost the World Series to the Dodgers in 1965. We had a good, solid, young team that figured to keep improving. I looked at the opposition and was convinced that we would win again—if not the next year, then certainly the year after. I was sure we had the kind of team that could get to the World Series two or three more times in the next five or six years, especially because the Yankees were rapidly on the decline.

As it turned out, after 1965, the next time I made it back to baseball's big show was four teams and 17 years later.

I had my best year in 1966. I led the league with 25 wins—the only time I won 20 games with the Twins—with a 2.75 ERA, completed 19 of my 41 starts, and pitched three shutouts. I probably would have won my only Cy Young Award, if they had given one in the American League. Unfortunately, they were giving only one Cy Young Award for both leagues, and Sandy Koufax, predictably and deservedly, won it with his 27 wins, 1.75 ERA, and 317 strikeouts. It wasn't until the following year that they started giving one Cy Young Award in each league.

It was a disappointment to me to have had my best year and not reach the World Series. We finished second to Baltimore, and the reason they beat us out for the American League pennant by nine games can be summed up in two words—*Frank Robinson*. He had come over to the Orioles from the Reds in one of the best baseball trades ever (one of the worst from Cincinnati's point of view). Frank won the triple crown—a .316 average, 49 home runs, 122 RBIs—and carried the Orioles to the pennant.

After that, we tied for second in 1967 and seventh in 1968. It wasn't until 1969, when Billy Martin took over as manager, that we won again.

I touched every part of Billy's career. He came to us as a player in 1961, and in his first game, we broke a 12-game losing streak. I pitched a complete game, and he hit a three-run homer against Baltimore. I had my picture taken with him after the game. He was the hitting star and I was the pitching star, so I got off to a good start with Martin. I thought that was pretty cool stuff. Here's Billy Martin, the former Yankees World Series hero, and he's my teammate.

Then he became a scout and a coach for the Twins under Sam Mele, and our relationship got a little strained because I was aligned with pitching coach Johnny Sain and Billy sided with Mele against Sain. When the Twins fired Sain, I wrote an editorial in support of John that ran in the *Minneapolis Star*, and that didn't help my relationship with Mele or Martin.

Billy was the kind of guy who if you stood up to him, he'd respect that and give you your space. When he took over as manager in Minnesota, Billy had two pitching coaches, Early Wynn and Art Fowler. Wynn had a contract and the organization was committed to him, and Fowler went wherever Billy went.

The winter before Martin took over, I had lunch with him and he said, "Fowler's your pitching coach," which I took as a compliment because I knew Art was Billy's guy. It also pleased me because Wynn liked to run his pitchers, but Fowler was just the opposite. He used to say, "Jesse Owens never won any games. Why should pitchers run?"

I didn't like to do a lot of running. I don't believe in it. Legs are important for a pitcher, but I believe a pitcher gets his legs in shape to pitch by pitching, fielding ground balls, shagging fly balls in the outfield, and spending a lot of time using his legs on the mound.

I was with the Yankees in 1979, the year Goose Gossage got into the clubhouse fight with Cliff Johnson and tore ligaments in his thumb. While he was inactive, Goose would go out running every day—running, running, running—and he kept saying what great shape he was in. I said, "Wait until you get in a game. You use your legs differently when you pitch." Gossage was reactivated, and they brought him into a game in Anaheim. We had a three-run lead, and Goose got through the first inning and then went out for his second inning. He gave up a home run, so it's a two-run lead. Goose went out for the ninth inning and gave up a solo home run, then a two-run home run, and we lost the game.

We came back to the clubhouse and Goose was sitting in front of his locker, huffing and puffing. He was exhausted. I walked over to him and said, "Hey, Goose, how do your legs feel?" He wanted to chase me around the locker room.

The point is, I don't care how much you run. I'd rather spend 25 to 30 minutes pushing off the rubber, using my legs that way. Sain always said the reason pitching coaches run their pitchers is that they don't have a lot to tell them about pitching.

The thing I enjoyed about pitching for Martin is that he'd let you pitch forever. That spring, my last start in spring training, Lou Brock hit a line drive back at me, and I knocked it down and lunged for it and felt something in my groin. Two days later, we broke camp to start the season and my groin was tightening up and it was sore. I was having a hard time just walking. I was scheduled to pitch the third game of the season in Kansas City, and Billy saw me limping around and said, "You going to be all right?"

"I think so," I said. "I'm going to give it a try."

He said, "Maybe you can give us five."

I came out of the game after 11 innings, tied, 4–4. I was walking on one leg. That's the way Billy was with his pitchers. If you were getting the job done, he'd let you go. From that standpoint, I liked pitching for him because you were never going to get a quick hook.

The reverse was that Martin was such a second-guesser. He just killed catchers. If a catcher didn't call a curveball, Billy would be all over him. We had a pact with our catchers that if we gave up a home run on a fastball and Billy came running out to the mound and challenged it—"What did you throw? It looked like a fastball"—we'd say, "No, it was a slider. It just hung. It was flat."

You'd have to do that with Martin just to protect the catcher and keep peace.

One time I pitched on a Friday night and on Sunday we had a doubleheader in Seattle. It was my day to throw, so Billy came to me—he'd do this often with me because he didn't have many left-handers—and asked me, "Can you give me anything?"

"Sure," I said.

I was brought into the game in the tenth inning, and I was still in there in the sixteenth.

It was only two days after I had started, and I was in my sixth inning. If a manager did that today, the pitcher's agent would be on the telephone threatening to file a grievance. Anyway, I faced Jim Pagliaroni in the sixteenth inning. It must have been about a nine- or ten-pitch at-bat. I threw him a few slow curves, a little of this, a little of that. Everything I had. I finally thought I had him where I could get a fastball past him on the hands. It was a mistake. He didn't hit it well, but he got enough of it and got it out of the old Seattle ballpark, and we lost the game.

The next day, Art Fowler came to me at my locker and said, "Billy thought you should have thrown him a curveball."

I went ballistic. I marched right into Martin's office and told him, "If you want to call my pitches before I throw them, that's fine, but don't send Artie over to my locker after the game is over to tell me I should have thrown a curveball."

I could talk to Billy like that. As I said, if you stood up to him, he respected you and left you alone. We got on fine from that standpoint. One time in Oakland, I got knocked out in the fourth inning in the first game. In the second game, they scored a run off Ron Perranoski and tied the score, and Billy asked me, "Can you give me an inning or two?" I said, "Yeah." I wound up pitching eight innings, almost a complete game in the second game of a doubleheader after I had pitched four innings in the first game. That part of it I liked. I liked pitching for Billy because I liked to pitch.

Running a game, I thought Billy was brilliant. He always forced the other team's hand. To this day, there are plays Martin originated that are still used by managers. There was in particular that we called "Bob White, Broken Wing." First and third, one out, and a left-handed hitter, who was having trouble hitting, coming up. Billy would have already told him to drag bunt the ball past the mound toward second base. Even if they got one out, you're going to get a run home. Or runners on first and third with less then two outs, he would have the runner from first break for second, then fall down between first and second. While the other team is tagging out the guy on first, the runner would score from third.

The year Billy took over as manager of the Twins, 1969, was the year the American League expanded to 12 teams and went to division play for the first time. Martin took a team that had won 79 games and finished seventh the previous year and won 97 games and finished first in the American League West. He had Rod Carew steal home seven times that year, still a major league record.

Billy had a reputation for ruining pitchers, but that year he had two 20-game winners—Jim Perry, who had never won 20 before, and Dave Boswell, whose best year before that was 14 wins and who never won close to 20 again. Yes, the same Boswell who was beaten up by Martin in one of the many fights that helped him earn his reputation as "Battling Billy."

It was in Detroit. That night, the pitchers were supposed to get in their running, but Bos didn't run. After the game, some of the players, Billy, and the coaches went over to the Lindell A.C., which

58

was a popular players' hangout. I wasn't there, but I heard about it. Martin and Fowler were sitting at the bar, and Boswell was at the pool table, and Fowler made the comment to Billy, "Boswell didn't feel good enough to run, but it sure looks like he feels OK now."

By this time, Billy obviously had had a few drinks, and when he was drinking, he got pugnacious. He confronted Boswell. Bos went after Fowler because Art ratted on him. From that point on, what happened depends on whose story you believe. Billy led everybody to believe he beat up Boswell, one-on-one. I saw Bos the next morning, and he had black-and-blue marks all over his face. I asked him what happened, and he said, "Billy had a couple of his boys hold me in the back of the Lindell, and while they were holding me, Billy punched me."

My inclination is to believe Boswell's story. To me, there's no way Billy could take Boswell one-on-one. Boswell was four inches taller, 25 pounds heavier, and 17 years younger than Martin. In my mind, Billy could not have done that kind of damage to Bos if he didn't have help.

That was only one incident. There were others that led to Billy's downfall in Minnesota and got him fired after one year, even though he improved the team and won the division. But that was his history. He'd take over a team, improve it immediately, then before very long, he'd get into a fight or defy authority and wear out his welcome. It happened in Minnesota, in Detroit, in Texas, in Oakland, and in New York. In New York, it happened several times.

Billy was the manager of the Yankees when I went over there in 1979. He still had that brilliant baseball mind, still was good at running the game, but he had changed. He had been through the wars with George Steinbrenner, and he wasn't very responsible. He would show up late for games. My problems with him in New York were the same ones I had with him in Minnesota.

That was the year Thurman Munson was killed when he crashed his private plane practicing takeoffs and landings at Canton Airport. That was the saddest time I ever experienced in baseball, the memorial to Munson at Yankee Stadium on the night after he died, the funeral in Canton, and playing the game on the night of the funeral. It was heart wrenching.

A few days after that happened, the Yankees brought up a young catcher from the minor leagues named Brad Gulden. Gulden was catching, and I came in to face a left-handed hitter, who was taken out for a pinch-hitter, Al Cowens, a right-handed hitter. Billy said, "You throw this guy breaking balls. Curveballs."

I knew Billy was going to say that because he always said the same thing in Minnesota. He was in love with the curveball. Billy left and I told Brad, "You give me a curveball sign so that you've done your job, but I'm going to shake you off. I'm not throwing Cowens a curveball. I need a double play and my curveball is not a ground ball pitch. I'm going to throw him a sinking fastball."

Gulden gave me the sign for the curve; I shook him off and threw a fastball. But I didn't get it out far enough, and Cowens hit it down the right-field line for a hit. Here came Billy out of the dugout.

"What was that pitch?"

"A fastball," Gulden said.

Billy started chewing out Gulden, and I was trying to get between them, but Billy kept pushing me away and getting in Gulden's face. He wouldn't even listen to me. Finally, I tapped him on the shoulder and said, "Billy, the kid called for a curve. I shook him off. I wanted to throw a fastball because that's my double-play pitch."

And Billy said, "The catcher's in charge. It's his fault."

He just buried Gulden, which is what he always did to catchers.

Another problem I had with Billy was his dishonesty. In 1969, my dad had a stroke and was in the hospital. I had pitched nine innings in Cleveland on a Saturday, and we were scheduled to go to Milwaukee on Monday to play an exhibition game against the Giants, then on to Minnesota on Tuesday. I asked Billy if it was all right for me to go to Michigan to see my dad and miss the exhibition game. I wasn't going to pitch anyway, and I'd rejoin the team in time for the game Tuesday in Minnesota. These days, players take off when their wife is giving birth or if there's an illness in their family, and that's good. It was different back then. You had to ask for permission, and often you wouldn't get it. But Billy said, "Sure, go ahead."

I waited until after the game on Sunday—I wouldn't think about leaving before the game even though I wasn't going to pitch that day—and I drove to Michigan. When I got to Minnesota, Ruthie Stewart, Calvin Griffith's secretary, called my house and said, "The boss would like you to come in early today. He wants to see you."

I went to Griffith's office and he started chewing me out. "Nobody does that," he said. "Nobody jumps my club. Nobody leaves without permission."

What had happened was it had rained in Milwaukee and they wanted to get the player representatives together to decide how long we would wait before they called off the game. Jim Davenport was the player rep for the Giants, and I was the player rep for the Twins. Calvin came into the clubhouse looking for me. He asked Billy, "Where's Kaat?" Billy said, "I guess he missed the plane."

I told Griffith that I asked Martin for permission to visit my father in the hospital and he said it was OK. By this time, Calvin was beginning to put two and two together because this kind of thing was happening a lot with Billy.

61

I think one of Billy's big problems was he wanted everybody to like him. He wanted to be the good guy. That's why he'd give me permission to leave the team to see my father, but then he didn't back me.

The last straw for Billy with Calvin Griffith was the American League Championship Series against Baltimore in 1969. Calvin called Martin into his office and asked him who he was going to pitch in the playoffs. Billy said Jim Perry, Dave Boswell, and Bob Miller. Griffith wanted me to pitch the third game, and they got into it over that. We were swept in three games, and Miller didn't last two innings in the third game. That didn't go over well with Calvin, but it was just one of many examples where Billy defied Griffith, and that's what got him fired.

Looking back, that was inevitable with Billy. He'd improve a team, and the fans loved him. But somewhere along the line, he'd defy his bosses and wear out his welcome and get fired. It happened to him many times.

CHAPTER

The "Old Timer" and the "Hard Hat"

Billy Martin was fired after one year as manager of the Minnesota Twins and was replaced by Bill Rigney in 1970. Our first season under Rigney was practically a carbon copy of the previous season under Billy. Once again we finished first in the American League West, by nine games over Oakland. Once again we faced the Baltimore Orioles in the American League Championship Series. And once again, we lost to the Orioles in a three-game sweep.

This time, I got a chance to pitch. I started the third game, lasted two innings, gave up two runs, and was the losing pitcher. After going 14–10 in the regular season, losing the playoff game was a big disappointment.

From that point, the Twins went into a decline. We finished fifth in 1971 and third in 1972. Harmon Killebrew, now in his upper thirties, was coming to the end of his fabulous career. Zoilo Versalles

63

never was able to duplicate his Most Valuable Player season of 1965 and was traded after the 1967 season with Mudcat Grant to the Los Angeles Dodgers for John Roseboro, Ron Perranoski, and Bob Miller. Bob Allison retired in 1971. Several operations on his knees would rob Tony Oliva of a certain Hall of Fame career. He won his third batting title in 1971 but played in only 10 games in 1972 and sadly never batted .300 again.

Rod Carew arrived in 1967 and would become the premier average hitter in the American League with seven batting titles, six of them from 1972 to 1978. When the era of free agency came along, the ever-frugal Twins, unable or unwilling to pay the escalating salaries, lost several players to other teams and traded Carew rather than paying him what he deserved.

In 1971, my record dropped to 13–14, but I bounced back the next year and was on my way to having my best year in some time. I was 10–2 with a 2.07 ERA when I broke my wrist sliding into second base and missed the entire second half. The next year, I began to get bad vibes that my days in Minnesota were numbered. I was in my midthirties, my salary had crept up to the princely sum of $60,000, and I had battled Calvin Griffith every year at contract time. Because of that, I clearly was not one of Griffith's pets, and I knew he would move me when the opportunity presented itself.

That opportunity came late in the 1973 season. Marv Grissom, the Twins' pitching coach, asked me if I would be content to pitch once a week, be a spot starter, and work out of the bullpen. And I thought, no, I wouldn't be content to do that. I felt I could still pitch, and I thought I had proved that before I broke my wrist. I was just getting back to where I had been, and that's when the Twins put me on waivers. It was a shock. The word was that either the Yankees or the Royals, each in contention and looking for a veteran left-handed starter, was going to claim me. If I got through waivers, I would go to one of those two teams, and in return, the Twins would get a young player or, more to Griffith's liking, money above the waiver price.

Before the Yankees or the Royals could get me, several other teams had to pass on me. Surprisingly, the White Sox, who had first dibs, put in a claim for me. They were about 15 games out of first place at the time, but they took me for $20,000. I was on the golf course in Minnesota when it happened. I got a message that Roland Hemond, general manager of the White Sox, was on the phone.

"We just claimed you," Hemond said. "You're the first player under the 5 and 10 rule, and you can refuse the deal if you want."

I wasn't aware of that. It was a new rule, won by the Players Association in the latest collective bargaining agreement: a player with 10 years of major league service, the last 5 years with the same team, had the right to refuse a trade. At the time, I was in my 15th major league season, all with the Washington Senators/Minnesota Twins.

"We're looking ahead to next year," Hemond said. "We think you've got some good years left. We'll give you a contract for next year for $70,000."

The money is different today; with the multimillion-dollar salaries, today's players might not identify with this, but I thought, "I'm making $60,000 with the Twins and I'm close to getting released. If I did stay with Minnesota, they'd cut my salary. And here's a team that wants to give me a $10,000 raise. Of course I'll accept this trade. I want to go where I'm wanted."

I went to Chicago where I was reunited with my old pitching coach, Johnny Sain, which was a bonus for me. I truly believe it was Sain who talked to White Sox manager Chuck Tanner about getting me.

When I got to Chicago, I worked with Sain and threw every day, 10 days in a row, and then I took a few days off and Chuck said, "We're going to start you against Detroit."

I went 4–1 the rest of the year, so I finished the season a combined 15–13 with Minnesota and Chicago.

The next year, 1974, I started out 4–1, but I didn't deserve to be 4–1. I was getting hammered. The next thing I knew, it started catching up with me. I went to 4–6. I couldn't get anybody out. Harry Caray, the great Cardinals, White Sox, and Cubs Hall of Fame broadcaster, was killing me on the air. "Folks," he said, "when your fastball and your slow curve are the same speed, it's time to call it a career. I don't know what in the world Chuck keeps running him out there for. We got Carl Moran and Skip Pitlock in the bullpen." Harry was just burying me.

We got off a road trip and I was putting my suitcase in my car when I spotted Chuck walking over to me. I thought, "He's going to call me in tomorrow and that will be it." He came up to me and said, "You've been averaging 15 wins a year in this league for 15 years. There's nothing wrong with you physically. There's no reason you can't still be a winning pitcher. I'm going to put you in the bullpen for about a week. You throw every day like you always did. I'll use you if I need you, but I'm going to start you in two weeks against Cleveland."

A few days later, Chuck brought me out of the bullpen and I got one of those cheap wins where I got two outs, we scored a bunch of runs, and I was the winning pitcher. I went back into the rotation and ended up 21–13. The following year I was 20–14. I was 35 at the time. These days, 35 is young for a pitcher, but back then it was considered ancient. Another manager might have said, "You're 35 years old; you're at the end of your career." Chuck believed in me, and that's why I thank him for saving my career and why I say he was the best manager I ever had. If I had had any other manager but him in 1974, my career might have been over.

One of my teammates in Chicago was Dick Allen, who was one of my favorites. Dick had an adversarial relationship with the press, and when I found out I was going to be playing with him, I wondered what it was going to be like. It turned out to be a great experience. When I first got to Chicago, Dick was out with an ankle injury and he missed quite a bit of time. But the next year, we began bonding. We both liked horses, and we both liked baseball. He learned the game playing for Gene Mauch, and Dick was a guy you could sit with and talk about the inside of the game, which I often did.

Dick didn't care if he went four-for-four or oh-for-four; he was more interested in doing the little things you had to do to win the game. He could run the bases and play defense, and he could hit. Boy could he hit!

We got on well together. He liked that I worked fast, that I was into the game, and that I was always talking to my infielders. I'd say, "Heads up, now, this may be coming your way." Dick loved that. To this day, he tells people the two pitchers he most enjoyed playing behind were Bob Gibson and me.

Dick called me the "old timer" because I was the oldest guy on the team. Chuck used to let Dick have his way. On days when I was pitching, I would sit at my locker rubbing up the baseball, and a half hour before the game Dick would come sashaying in and he'd say, "Hey, old timer, you pitching tonight?"

"Yeah."

"Good, we'll be out of here in about an hour and 45 minutes."

Dick had come to the White Sox in 1972, the year before I got there, in a trade with the Dodgers for Tommy John. In 1971, the Sox had drawn about 800,000 fans and finished four games under .500. Dick turned things around. He batted .308 and led the league with 37 homers and 113 RBIs and was the Most Valuable Player. He carried that team almost single-handedly. He helped the White Sox make a run at Oakland, and he put people in the seats, so they began calling him "Mose," because like Moses, he almost led the White Sox to the Promised Land.

I had the good fortune to play with a few players I call legendary, like Harmon Killebrew and Pete Rose. I put Dick Allen in that category. He was truly legendary. He always wore the hard hat, even in the field. He would sit in the dugout before a game, wearing his hard hat and smoking a cigarette. Players would come filing into the dugout and look out at Comiskey Park, at the wind blowing straight in as it can only in Chicago, and some guy would say, "Nobody's going to hit one out of here tonight."

I'd look over at Dick and he'd give me a wink, and then the game would start and he'd go up there and . . . whoosh . . . he'd hit one into the upper deck.

I pitched a game in Cleveland where I had the bases loaded and nobody out, and I was already down, 1–0. There was a double-play ball, short to second to first. Dick had a habit of flipping the ball to the umpire after the third out. He got the ball to complete the double play and flipped it to the umpire. But the umpire jumped out of the way. Dick, who rarely made mistakes on the field, thought there were three outs. The runner from third scored, and the runner from second also came around and scored, so it was 3–0.

I got the side out and was coming off the field, and Dick said, "Sorry about that, old timer. I'll get those back for you."

He hit two three-run homers, and we won the game, 7–3.

Another time, I was pitching against the Angels and Nolan Ryan. Nobody even knew I was pitching because I was giving up two hits every inning and Ryan was pitching a no-hitter. I'd give up a couple of hits and somebody would hit into a double play. Another hit, another double play. I must have given up 9 or 10 hits, but we were only down 1–0 going into the bottom of the ninth inning, and Ryan still had his no-hitter with about 11 or 12 strikeouts.

Dick was going to lead off the ninth, and as we ran off the field, he said, "Old timer, we're going to win this game."

He hit a two-hopper to third baseman Rudy Meoli, who picked it up, figured he had enough time, gave it an extra look, took a hop and a step, and then threw to first. Zoom! Dick beat the throw for an infield hit. There was a bunt, a throwing error, a bloop hit, and a sacrifice fly and we won the game, 2–1.

That was Dick Allen. He could do it all. He cared so much about playing the game the right way, it bothered him to see players who didn't play the game fundamentally right and didn't do the little things necessary to win. He had a hard time accepting that not everybody approached the game the way he did.

Dick could be charming and he could be aloof. He was many things to many people and he wasn't easily impressed with celebrity, his own or another's.

One day in the 1974 season, Elliott Gould came to Comiskey Park and asked to meet Dick. The public relations man arranged the meeting and brought Gould into our dugout before the game for the introductions. Dick was very gracious and friendly. After Gould left, Dick said, "Hey, old timer, who was that guy?"

"That's Elliott Gould," I said. "He's the star of that new movie, *M*A*S*H*. He used to be married to Barbra Streisand."

"Oh, yeah," Dick said. "Can he hit a slider?"

He was an enigma. I've scratched my head many times trying to figure out what made him tick. He could do so many things on a ball field, but he was traded so many times, probably because he marched to his own drummer. He wasn't a big rules guy, and maybe he rebelled against the game's structure. He didn't like being told this is what you have to do and this is when you have to do it. He wouldn't take batting practice, yet he would hit 35 home runs and knock in 120. Chuck Tanner was the right manager for him. Chuck's philosophy was 25 players, 25 different sets of rules. I'll handle everybody differently.

Dick was special, and he was legendary, but he didn't want to follow rules, and he wasn't the most responsible guy. Where that came from, I don't know. I can't condone everything Dick did and was allowed to get away with. He was puzzling because he had Hall of Fame ability and never fully reached that potential.

Later, we were teammates again in Philadelphia. He had a little influence with Phillies owner Ruly Carpenter, and when they were looking for a veteran left-hander, Dick suggested they get me. I was traded over there before the 1976 season.

My All-Teammates Team

I was fortunate throughout my career to have had so many great players behind me when I pitched. Some, like Harmon Killebrew, were great offensive players. Others, like Ozzie Smith, were great defensive players. And some, like Mike Schmidt and Tony Oliva, were great offensively *and* defensively. In choosing my all-time greatest team of players I played with, I have a mixture of offensive and defensive players because, while a pitcher appreciates plays behind him that bail him out of jams, he also knows you need runs to win games.

If I hedge a bit, or select more than one player at a position, it's because there have been so many outstanding teammates to choose from, I want to make certain not to overlook anybody. For that reason, I also want to include a utility player on my team, and for that job I'm selecting my old Twins teammate Cesar Tovar, who could play all over the place. In fact, in one game, he did play all nine positions and he struck out Reggie Jackson.

Here, then, is my all-time team of those who were my teammates:

Catcher: Earl Battey was the catcher in my formative years, the first six years of my big-league career. He was a calming influence because he was very quiet behind the plate. He had a great arm and a good sense of humor. He wasn't a high-energy guy who would come out there to get you riled up. He kept it simple. He was perfect for me at that stage of my career, and we hit it off well as friends and as pitcher and catcher.

Earl would come down to warm me up in the bullpen the last few minutes to get a feel for what I had that day, and when I was finished, just to keep me loose, he'd say, "You're not going out there with that stuff, are you?"

That's the sort of thing one teammate can say to another without any hard feelings. It's just clubhouse humor. Tough love. For example, I had a teammate named Lenny Green who we called "Pea Head" because he had a small head. He was a lovable and classy guy from Detroit and a great teammate. One day I was knocked out early in a game and I was headed to the clubhouse to shower and dress. Lenny came over and said, "Hey, kid, don't use all the hot water."

A few starts later, as I was about to take the mound, Lenny passed me on his way to the outfield and said, "Hey, kid, stick around long enough to shower with the boys today."

Another time I gave up a mammoth home run to Mickey Mantle. After the game Ray Moore, a veteran pitcher, came to my locker and put his hand on my shoulder in what I thought was a consoling gesture.

"How'd you grip that pitch?" he asked.

I showed him and Ray said, "Don't grip it like that again."

Moore is the same guy who offered to buy me a steak dinner after I had two teeth knocked out by a line drive back to the mound.

After Battey left, I had John "Gabby" Roseboro for about a year and a half. Gabby was a lot like Battey. I'd be pitching to Mickey Mantle in a close game with Elston Howard on deck. If I fell behind in the count, 2–0, I wouldn't want to walk Mantle, so Roseboro would give me the sign for a fastball and make the sign of the cross and just sit right there in the middle of the plate.

I want to include Phil Roof, who never gets mentioned among the game's great catchers but was my personal catcher with the Twins in 1972. We were roommates and great friends, even though I had to hit him in the ribs with a pitch when he was with Kansas City. Harmon Killebrew was trying to score from second. Roof blocked the plate and stuck his knee out. Killer went flying, and Roofie went over and tagged him.

It upset everybody in our dugout. They were yelling, "He's got to go," and I was pitching, so the next inning I drilled him in the ribs. Four years later, he was my teammate.

First Base: This is my one big dilemma. I want Dick Allen and Keith Hernandez both on my all-time team, and I can't separate them. Dick was a great teammate and a great hitter. He wasn't in Hernandez's class defensively, but he was pretty good. Keith wasn't in Dick's class offensively, but he was a great defensive first baseman, the best I ever saw at fielding bunts and going to third base. Rarely do pitchers hang with hitters; they'll hang with other pitchers or with catchers. Dick and Keith were two guys with whom I had great relationships on and off the field.

Second Base: Rod Carew is a Hall of Famer and a great hitter. He wasn't as good defensively as Tommy Herr, whom I played with in St. Louis and was an excellent second baseman on both sides of the ball: a switch-hitter, good on the double play, a real solid player. But if I'm pitching Game 7 of the World Series and I get to pick who I want behind me, it would be Rod Carew.

Shortstop: In 1965, Zoilo Versalles was the American League MVP. He was an offensive force, but he didn't have the length of career of a Larry Bowa or an Ozzie Smith. I was with Bowa in Philadelphia, and he was an outstanding shortstop. I loved to have him behind me when I pitched. But when it's all said and done, I'd take Ozzie Smith. He did things nobody did.

I always took pride in my reflexes. If a ground ball was hit through the middle, I'd get it. When I got to St. Louis, my 40-year-old reflexes weren't quite what my 25-year-old reflexes had been. There'd be a guy on first and a ground ball would be hit through the middle, and I'd reach for it and just miss it. I'd go to back up third base and I'd turn around, and there was Ozzie turning it into a 6-4-3 double play. I had to pitch with him behind me to appreciate how many runs he saved.

Third Base: Mike Schmidt. There's no argument here. I had Graig Nettles for a short time, but he got traded and never had the chance to show how good he was defensively with the Twins as he did with the Yankees. Most of the third basemen I played with were offensive-minded, like Harmon Killebrew and Rich Rollins in Minnesota and Bill Melton in Chicago.

Schmidt was great on both offense and defense. He loved to be involved in the whole game. He would come to the mound and say, "You gotta curve this guy. He really sits on the fastball." I'd let a few seconds go by and say, "Schmidty, you're the greatest third baseman I've ever played with. Now just get back there and play it."

He was unbelievable. Once in St. Louis, where the visiting bullpen was down the third-base line, we had a one-run lead in the bottom of the ninth, and the tying run was on third base. Reggie Smith, batting right-handed, hit a rocket down the third-base line, the ball zipping on artificial turf. Schmidty darted to his right and backhanded the ball. When he did, he was looking right at us in the bullpen and he winked. Then he came up and threw a pea to first to end the game. That's how cool Schmidty was. And you know about all the home runs he hit, 548 of them.

Right Field: I told you how much respect I have for Tony Oliva, but don't take my word for it. Ask the catchers of that era—Andy Etchebarren, Bill Freehan, Larry Haney, Bob Montgomery. In a lineup that had Killebrew, Carew, and Oliva, those catchers would tell you that while they had great respect for Killebrew and Carew, the one guy they didn't want to see come up in a crucial situation was Oliva. There just was no way to pitch him.

That speaks highly of Oliva, who is the right fielder on my all-time teammates team, and not just for his offense. Here's a guy who, when he was young and they would hit him fly balls, couldn't put leather on the ball. Two years later, he won a Gold Glove.

Center Field: In Philadelphia, I played with Garry Maddox, who had the ability to play shallow and still catch everything hit out there. There were times when line drives were hit that I actually jumped for and Maddox caught at his shoe tops. Yet he went back on balls as well as anybody I've ever seen. They called him the "Secretary of Defense" in Philadelphia. Ralph Kiner came up with the classic line, "Two-thirds of the world is covered by water and the rest is covered by Garry Maddox."

Left Field: While I was in Philadelphia, Allen Lewis, a longtime and respected baseball writer, told me, "Your old teammate Harmon Killebrew is eligible for the Hall of Fame, but I'm not going to vote for him on the first ballot."

I asked why and he said, "All he was was a home-run hitter."

I said, "Well, he hit 573 of them and with you being in the National League, what you didn't appreciate is that he hit them in clutch situations against tough pitchers."

In 1965, when we were still fearful of the Yankees, we played them in a four-game series in Minnesota in July. We had a two-game lead in the standings and won two of the first three in the series, but if we lost the fourth game, our lead in the standings would have been back to only two.

We were down by a run and Harmon came up with two out in the ninth inning and a man on against Pete Mikkelsen, who kept the ball down and was tough to hit out of the ballpark. Killer must have fouled off eight or nine pitches, then he hit the ball out and we won the game. It was one of the most memorable home runs in my Minnesota career.

Killebrew was that kind of hitter. He was such a force late in the game that Dick Williams, when he managed in Oakland, would tell Rollie Fingers to stay home, not come out for the game, because he didn't want Rollie pitching to Killebrew, who just wore out Fingers.

Killer wasn't much of a defensive player, and he never hit for a high average. I put him in left for his bat and because he was such a great teammate and I'd want him on my team in case I needed a two-run homer in the ninth to win the game.

CHAPTER 9

A Trip to the Bronx Zoo

After 17 years in the major leagues, I finally made it to the city of my father's favorite team, Philadelphia. It wasn't the Athletics—they were long gone to Kansas City—but it was close enough.

I enjoyed my time in Philly. I joined a veteran team that was a National League power, always in contention, with players like Dick Allen, Mike Schmidt, Greg Luzinski, Larry Bowa, Bob Boone, Tim McCarver, Steve Carlton, Jim Lonborg, and Tug McGraw. We had a good team and a good group of guys. We were very close and, in fact, I still stay in touch with most of them. While my time with the Phillies was good personally, it was a disappointment professionally.

I had won 41 games in the two previous seasons in Chicago. In 1975, at the age of 36, I won 20 games, started 41, and pitched more than 300 innings. When the trade was made, Chuck Tanner told Danny Ozark, the Phillies manager, "You've got to pitch him a lot."

Ozark did just the opposite. He said, "I'm going to hold you out against Montreal; they've got all those right-handed hitters."

"Yeah," I said. "I've only faced about nine thousand of them in my career. I must have got some of them out."

I felt bad because in my time there, Philadelphia didn't get the best out of me. I had a pretty good year in 1976. My record was deceptive. I was only 12–14, but if you ask anybody, I pitched better than that. I could have been 16–10. I lost a couple of 1–0 games. I was the guy that year—there's always one on any pitching staff—who didn't get a lot of runs to work with.

We won the National League East and faced Cincinnati's Big Red Machine—Bench, Perez, Rose, Morgan, and the rest—in the National League Championship Series. We had the lead in all three games, and the Reds came back to win all three.

We won the National League East again in 1977 and again were knocked out in the playoffs, this time by the Dodgers. In 1978, the same thing. We won the NL East and got knocked out by the Dodgers in the NLCS.

By 1979, I knew I was on my way out of Philadelphia. I was not one of Ozark's favorites. We got along fine, but I was not a hard thrower and he had no confidence in me. I was on the team, and he had to have me there, but he wouldn't use me. If I started a game and a man got on base in the first inning, I'd look over my shoulder and they were already warming somebody up in the bullpen.

To try to keep sharp, I'd get up every night in the bullpen with Bob Tiefenauer, our bullpen coach, looking on, and I'd throw to Dave Rader, our backup catcher. I'd pitch a simulated game. I'd look up at the scoreboard and say, "I'm pitching against the Red Sox tonight; they've got Lynn, Rice, Evans, Hobson." When the inning started, I began throwing in the bullpen like I was pitching a four- or five-inning game. That was the only time I could get any work to try to stay sharp.

One night in San Diego, I got up and had been throwing for about 20 minutes when Ozark called down to Tiefenauer and said, "Tell him to sit down." Wouldn't you know we tied the game off Rollie Fingers and went into extra innings. Ozark had used up his bullpen. I was the last option. We went into the eleventh inning and they called down and I was in the game. I pitched four innings and got the win.

After the game, Ozark said, "It's a good thing you pitched good tonight with all that throwing you did in the bullpen."

I said, "Danny, if I didn't do all that throwing in the bullpen, I probably wouldn't have been able to hit the backstop."

Birdie Tebbetts was at the game that night scouting for the Yankees. It was right about the time Rich Gossage had gotten into a clubhouse fight with Cliff Johnson and Gossage tore a ligament in his thumb and was on the disabled list. Ron Guidry had volunteered to replace Gossage as the Yankees' closer, so they were short a starting pitcher. They needed a warm body, a left-hander in the bullpen.

The Phillies went from San Diego to San Francisco, and that's when they told me, "The Yankees picked up your contract on the waiver list." It was May 11, 1979, a Friday.

We had a bridge club in Philadelphia—Tim McCarver, Jim Lonborg, Mike Schmidt, Gary Maddox, Davey Johnson, and me. We kept a record of the points. Schmidty was always behind. If he was minus 350 points, he'd have to put $350 in the pot and we'd all go out and have dinner. That's what we did on my last night as a Phillie. We went to dinner with the money from our bridge club, and then I caught the red-eye from San Francisco to New York and joined the Yankees on a Saturday.

It was with mixed emotions that I arrived at Yankee Stadium. As a boy, I rooted for the Philadelphia Athletics and hated the Yankees as most Midwesterners did. You hated the Yankees and you hated Notre Dame because they always won. You wanted to see them get knocked off. But as an adult, a longtime major leaguer who was fascinated with and passionate about this game, I was thrilled to be wearing the pinstripes and to be playing in baseball's cathedral with all its history and tradition.

Looking back, having been a part of the Yankees franchise all these years as a player and a broadcaster, knowing what I know now, there's nothing like playing in New York. When you experience their tradition and you see what they do for their players, you understand how special it is to be a Yankee.

I also arrived with curiosity because of all the stuff that went down with Billy and George, George and Thurman, Thurman and Reggie, Reggie and Billy. I was going to a team that had won the previous two World Series, but when I joined them, they were in trouble. There was the Gossage injury, and Thurman Munson was hurting and it looked like he was coming to the end of his career as a catcher. The Orioles had gotten off to a fast start and the Yankees were sliding, trying to hold things together.

I arrived in New York and there wasn't time to go to the hotel, so I went straight from the airport to Yankee Stadium. Bob Lemon, the manager, greeted me with, "Welcome to the Bronx Zoo. Can you pitch?"

"Yeah," I said. "I pitched a few innings a couple of nights ago, but I'm fine."

My first day as a Yankee, just off the red-eye from San Francisco, with hardly any sleep, I came into the game and the first batter I faced while I was wearing a Yankees uniform was my old teammate

Dad drove all the way from our hometown of Zeeland, Michigan, to Cooperstown in 1948 for the Hall of Fame induction of Lefty Grove, who was his favorite player—until I came along.

My first championship: the Zeeland Lions, 1949 playground champs. I'm second from the left, bottom row.

The 1957 Superior Senators, my first professional team. That's me, at age 18, fourth from the left on the top row.

I got to see a good part of the western United States in this crate with the Missoula Timberjacks in 1958, my first full season as a professional.

Pitching for the Missoula Timberjacks in the Class C Pioneer League in 1958. My manager and catcher was "Trader Jack" McKeon.

I was the ace left-hander of the Chattanooga Lookouts of the Southern League in 1959. Next stop: Washington.

In 1959 I was a Washington Senator for only three games—no threat to Strom Thurmond's tenure.

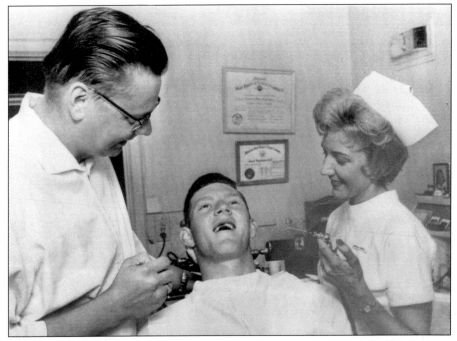

In 1962 I lost two teeth and part of a third when I was struck in the mouth by a line drive off the bat of Detroit's Bubba Morton. It made me work hard to improve my fielding. Photo courtesy of Bettman/CORBIS.

I was thrilled in 1965 when I learned I would start Game 2 of the World Series against Sandy Koufax, who was the greatest pitcher I ever saw. Photo courtesy of Bettman/CORBIS.

This photo was taken in 1965 in my hometown of Zeeland, Michigan. Mom and Dad always were my biggest fans—and I was theirs.

My dad gives me a handshake for good luck before Game 7 of the 1965 World Series, in Minneapolis. Photo courtesy of AP/Wide World Photos.

I had my best year in 1966 with the Twins. I led the American League in wins (25), starts (41), complete games (19), and innings pitched (304⅔), but I didn't win the Cy Young Award. There was only one award given for both leagues, and it went to Sandy Koufax.

Another Ford in my past (no, not Whitey). My son Jimmy and I met President Gerald Ford at the 1976 All-Star Game.

Rod Carew. The bases were loaded, and I got a double play and got out of the inning.

I have talked about playing with legendary players Harmon Killebrew, Pete Rose, and Dick Allen. In New York, I played with another one. Reggie Jackson was a legendary player. Just ask him.

The first time I ever set eyes on Reggie Jackson was at the end of the 1967 season when I was with the Minnesota Twins. We were in Kansas City to play the Athletics, and after a game, a few of us went to the Italian Gardens for dinner. Sitting in a corner of the restaurant were two young guys. From the looks of them, you could tell they were ballplayers, but I didn't recognize them.

I said, "Those two guys have to be ballplayers. They must have just been called up. Who are they?"

Somebody said, "That's Rick Monday and Reggie Jackson."

A day or two later, I was pitching and Reggie was in the starting lineup. We didn't have any detailed scouting report on him because he was new, but somebody said he heard this kid had good power to the opposite field, which was unusual in those days. Most guys that were home-run hitters pulled the ball. It was rare for a big power hitter to hit the ball out the opposite way. Even Harmon Killebrew, with his 573 home runs, probably didn't hit more than a handful to right field.

The first time I faced Reggie, I ran a fastball under his hands; he put his hands up to protect himself, and the ball hit the knob of the bat. I struck him out with a curve and I told my catcher, Earl Battey, we had to remember that. That's what you want to find out with a young hitter, if you can push him off the plate and then throw a pitch on the outside corner. From a personal standpoint, I used my first few encounters with Reggie to my advantage. I'd buzz Jackson inside, then I'd go away with a breaking ball and it frustrated him. One time, he even tried to bunt on me in a tie game.

He hit a few home runs off me, but I don't remember any that really hurt me. Still, it was fun to watch his career develop. He was like Roger Maris in the sense that when you think about Maris, you think about 61 home runs. He never got the credit for being the complete player he was. It was the same with Reggie. When you think about Reggie Jackson, you think about "Mr. October" and three home runs in the final game of the 1977 World Series.

When he was a kid, Reggie could run and he could throw, and what I always respected and admired about him was that he played hard. He once told my Yankees broadcast buddy, Ken Singleton, "You can like me or you can hate me, but you can't ignore me."

The impressive thing about Jackson was that he played hard every game. He had some showmanship, even when he was young. He was one of the first who would stand at home plate and admire his home runs. It wasn't like the guy was hitting only five home runs a year; he was a legitimate home-run hitter. Killebrew kind of did the same thing. Killer would stand there for an instant, then drop the bat and trot around the bases. Reggie did it with flair. He'd watch the ball and do a little dance and then circle the bases triumphantly.

By the time I hooked up with Jackson in New York, he had changed. We went out a few times and it always bothered me that he would be rude to people away from the field. So, I actually saw two Reggies. I saw this young, brash Reggie with all the talent in the world, and then I saw Reggie the superstar, who didn't seem to enjoy his success. Not like Kirby Puckett, for example. There's a guy who enjoyed his career. He was the same every day. He treated the 25th guy on the roster the same as he treated Kent Hrbek or Gary Gaetti. He was the same guy from the time he came up in 1984 until my last year broadcasting in Minnesota in 1993.

But Reggie didn't seem like he could be comfortable with people. He got an edge to him later on that he didn't have when he was a kid. It was disappointing to see his personality change.

One thing I'll never forget about that Yankees team was its wit. I wish I had a tape of the byplay that went on during the bus rides and plane trips. It was hilarious, with guys like Mickey Rivers, Oscar Gamble, Lou Piniella, Graig Nettles, and Catfish Hunter. It was a running, nonstop *Saturday Night Live*.

Rivers, "Mick the Quick," had a way of getting under Jackson's skin. Reggie is a very intelligent guy, and he would talk down to Mickey. He considered himself above Rivers. Reggie would say, "Mickey, don't you know I've got an IQ of 169?" And Mickey would come right back. "What's that, out of 1,000?"

Gamble was hitting ahead of Reggie at the time, and he'd say, "I can't get any pitches to hit. They're not pitching to me. They got Reggie coming up next and they know they're going to strike him out, so I can't get any pitches to hit. When I do get pitches to hit, I'm the ratio man." Oscar would come to bat 200 times, and he'd hit 20 home runs, or 1 homer for every 10 at-bats, so he called himself the "Ratio Man."

They could really ride herd on one another. Nettles had all these great one-liners like, "Most kids when they're little say they want to grow up to be a major league baseball player or be in the circus. I'm lucky. I got to do both."

Graig came through the Minnesota Twins and played with us briefly in 1967, 1968, and 1969, so he was one Yankee I knew pretty well. In fact, when Nettles came up at the end of the 1967 season, he was looking for a place to stay. There was Graig, his wife, Ginger, and their little dog, Ohfer, like oh for five, another example of Nettles' self-deprecating humor.

I had a room in the lower level of my house, kind of like a mother-in-law room, so I invited them to stay with us. It was going to be for only about a month. Graig accepted, and we developed a good friendship.

Eventually, Nettles got traded to Cleveland and his career took off. I had a tough time getting him out, and it might have been because we were such good friends. That happens a lot. It's not a conscious thing, but if a guy's your friend, he feels comfortable hitting against you. He was wearing me out, and one night when I was with the White Sox I was pitching against him in Chicago. All of a sudden he stepped out of the box because there was a moth or a butterfly flitting around him. He waved to shoo it away, then he looked out at me and said, with that typical Nettles wit, "I thought that was your fastball."

I can admit now that it was a funny line, but it wasn't funny to me at the time. I was fired up, competing in the game, and the remark got under my skin. I thought, "I'll show you my fastball." I buzzed the next pitch under his chin and he kind of looked at me like, "Wow!"

From then on, I started getting him out. I thought, "I should have done that in the first place."

Piniella and Hunter had a running feud going that had us in stitches. If they had taken their act on the cabaret circuit, they would have been a sensation. Catfish had signed the lucrative free-agent contract and Piniella was always on him about it, especially late in Catfish's career when it was becoming obvious that his arm had about had it and he was getting hammered pretty good. Lou would say, "Cat, man, this is not right. They put guys in jail for stealing $30 from a 7-Eleven, and you're walking around a free man, stealing the man's money."

One night when Hunter was pitching, Rivers went to his position in center field, and he turned his back to home plate and got into a sprinter's stance like he was getting ready to run to the outfield wall. It was all done in good fun. You could say and do those things to your teammate, but nobody else could do it. That's what made those trips so much fun and that team so special.

As much fun as that team was, the season turned into a disaster. Because of the Gossage injury and other factors, we dropped out of the race early. The Orioles had a terrific year and won 102 games, and we never could get it going. Lemon was fired and replaced by Billy Martin. And then there was the Thurman Munson tragedy, which I have said is the saddest thing I ever experienced in my baseball career.

One of the joys of my short tenure with the Yankees was playing with Thurman. I loved pitching to him. I was pitching middle relief and when I'd come in, he'd say, "Kitty, we're going to pitch 'bassackwards.' When we're ahead, we're going to throw fastballs. When we're behind, we're going to throw breaking balls."

I said, "That's pitching the right way. That's the way I like to pitch."

If there was a fastball hitter up, somebody like Eddie Murray, and I'd get to two strikes, Thurman would take great delight in giving me the sign for the fastball. It was a game to Thurman. He enjoyed trying to outthink the hitter, and I liked that.

Munson was a tough guy. He was beat up that year. His knees were aching and his shoulder was hurting so bad, he was throwing the ball sidearm. But he was a great competitor. He never complained, and he always played hard. And he was one of the great clutch hitters.

When I came to New York, I sublet an apartment near Central Park, right where Mickey Mantle's restaurant is now. It was the afternoon of Thursday, August 2. We had just come off a road trip to Milwaukee and Chicago and we had the day off before beginning a series at Yankee Stadium against Baltimore. I was in my apartment and I flipped on the television and heard the news. ". . . Yankees catcher Thurman Munson was killed today when his private plane crashed at Canton, Ohio, Airport. . . ."

I was stunned. I couldn't believe what I'd heard. I had just had dinner with Thurman in Chicago. Bucky Dent, Goose Gossage, and I, who had been teammates with the White Sox, liked to eat in this little Italian restaurant called Traverso's in suburban Chicago. The owners of the restaurant were big Yankees fans and big Munson fans. I told Thurman, "I'd love to take you out to this restaurant; they're big fans of yours. The restaurant will be closed and Mama Traverso will cook up whatever you want."

Munson agreed and we went out there on Tuesday night after the game. We had a lot of pasta, a little wine. We had a great time. Thurman loved it. He was in great spirits. The next night, we played the final game of the trip and flew back to New York and Thurman flew home to Canton. The next day, he was dead.

It was such a sad time. I had some friends who had come to New York for a few days. They would go to see a play or come to a game and then we'd go out to dinner, but I'm afraid I wasn't a very good host. I just walked around numb. And then there was the funeral in Canton. George Steinbrenner chartered a plane, and the whole team went to the funeral, which was heartbreaking. There was a motorcade and Lou Piniella and Bobby Murcer said eulogies that were so poignant and sad. Seeing Thurman's wife, Dianne, and his kids just tore your heart out. There were players there from other clubs—from the Indians and even some from the Orioles, like Rick Dempsey and Tippy Martinez.

Thurman was a unique individual. I'm sorry I didn't get to know him better and didn't get a chance to pitch to him longer. Going to the Yankees should have been a highlight of my career, but the death of Thurman Munson made it a bittersweet experience.

I left New York in 1980 with the George Washington, Triboro, and Whitestone Bridges burning behind me.

I was displeased with how the Yankees had led me along and then dumped me, and I knocked heads with the Boss, George Steinbrenner. I figured my chances of ever working in that city again were slim to none. I was the worm in the Big Apple.

I had appeared in 40 games for the Yankees in 1979, all but one of them in relief. I won two games, saved two, and had an ERA under 4, so I felt I had done my part to help the team, even though we finished well back of the Orioles. Billy Martin had replaced Bob Lemon as the manager, so at the end of the season I went into Billy and asked him, as I often did with my managers, "What do you think about next year?"

"Yeah," Billy said. "I want you back. I think you can still help us out of the bullpen. Go up and see George."

I made an appointment to see the Boss, and he was very cordial. I had been with the Yankees since May, but this was my first face-to-face meeting with Steinbrenner. Before I got there, I had heard all the stories about how, when he bought the club in 1973, he was quoted as saying, "I'm going to stick to building ships and let the baseball people run the baseball team."

I observed him from afar as one of three baseball owners, along with Ted Turner in Atlanta and Ray Kroc in San Diego, who were willing to spend money when free agency came along. I also heard stories about how when he first took over, he said, "Number 15 and number 28, I want them to get their hair cut," and that was Thurman Munson and Sparky Lyle.

After I got there, I saw Steinbrenner in the clubhouse occasionally, sat in on a few of his clubhouse meetings, and met him briefly in passing at a restaurant in Cleveland. But we had never had a one-on-one conversation until I went up to see him about my 1980 contract. I had heard he was tough to negotiate with, but I figured until I experienced that firsthand, I had no right to judge him. Now I was going to experience it firsthand.

I was making $150,000 and I really didn't have any numbers to throw at him, so Steinbrenner suggested a 13 percent cost-of-living increase, which brought me up to $168,000. "But," he said, "I've got some young players I want to protect on the roster, so I'm going to take you off the roster, then I'll put you back on after the waiver period, on December 1."

I agreed and went home after the season and waited for my contract. Instead, I got a letter from Gene Michael, who had taken over as general manager. The Yankees were inviting me to spring training to compete for a job as a nonroster player.

"Wait a minute," I thought. "That wasn't the deal I made with Steinbrenner."

I called Michael. "Didn't George tell you about our arrangement?"

"I don't know a thing about it," he said.

I called Steinbrenner's office in Tampa and got his secretary, who said, "I'll put you on his call list and he'll get back to you."

"I'll wait."

"It might be a while."

"I'll wait all day."

Steinbrenner got on the phone. "What's the problem?"

"Remember the conversation we had in September in your office at Yankee Stadium?"

88

He didn't remember a word about it, said it never happened. "I keep recordings of all my conversations," he said.

"George, I've been in this game a long time. If I didn't think I had a contract, I would have gone into the reentry draft."

He was adamant. "I don't remember a conversation," he insisted.

My hands were tied. The reentry draft was over, I had no other options, and so I reported to spring training as a nonroster player without a contract. I think maybe Steinbrenner remembered our conversation because he sent me a $5,000 bonus.

Martin was fired that winter after he punched a marshmallow salesman, and Dick Howser, who had been Martin's third-base coach, was named manager of the Yankees. The first thing I did when I got to spring training was go into the manager's office.

"Dick," I said, "I'm here because Billy wanted me back. If you have other ideas, let me know and I'll try to hook on with another team."

"No," Howser said. "I'm going to give you every chance to make the team."

"The only thing I'd like to ask, then, is since I have to earn my way on the team, pitch me when the regulars are playing: Bucky Dent, Graig Nettles, Willie Randolph, Chris Chambliss."

I figured if I was going to have to make the team, I didn't want to come into a game in the late innings when the regulars were out and the minor leaguers were playing. I wanted to give myself every chance to make the team. Howser was good about it. He even started me when it was my turn to pitch. I had a terrific spring. I pitched 19 scoreless innings. I'd pitch three innings, three up, three down, three up, three down. After I did that a couple of times, I went in to see Gene Michael.

"Stick," I said, "I'm 41 years old. What else do you need to see?"

"They want to take a look at you one more time."

No problem. I went out and pitched three or four more score-less innings. They were trying to find an excuse not to keep me, and I wasn't giving them one. Rudy May had a bad back and was put on the disabled list to start the season, so they had no choice but to keep me.

Stick called me into his office. "We're going to put you on the roster," he said. "Here's your contract."

It called for $150,000, the same salary I had made the year before.

"George and I agreed on $168,000."

Michael said he'd check into it and get back to me. We were in Clearwater for a game with the Phillies. I left Michael's office and went onto the field. A few minutes later, Stick came running out and called me over. "George said you sign that contract right now or he's going to take it off the table."

What choice did I have? I signed the contract for $150,000. Here's a guy who spends millions on free agents and he was chiseling me out of a paltry $18,000. I guess I was born too soon.

I started the season with the Yankees and pitched in only four games. Then Rudy May came off the disabled list and they put him on the roster. To make room for him, I was designated for assign-ment. The Cardinals picked me up.

Is it any wonder I was bitter with Steinbrenner and the Yankees? After I left, I exchanged a couple of letters and phone calls with Steinbrenner expressing my anger and disappointment at his con-venient lack of memory.

That was not to be my last go-round with George Steinbrenner.

My All-Opponents Team

My all-time opponents team, quite naturally, is stocked almost entirely with American League players, which is no knock on the National League. I played against a lot of great players in the National League, but it figures when you've played more than 20 of your 25 years in the American League, as I did, the players in that league are going to leave a more lasting impression.

As much as I admire players like Johnny Bench, Joe Morgan, Willie Mays, Willie McCovey, Roberto Clemente, Hank Aaron, Lou Brock, Billy Williams, and Willie Stargell, my body of work against them was not sufficient for their names to be included.

You'll notice, too, that my all-time opponents team is primarily an offensive array. That's also natural because, as a pitcher, I spent my career trying to get hitters out and, through the years, the following group of players caused me enough anguish and bumps and bruises to earn my utmost respect.

Catcher: Elston Howard. I was primarily a sinkerball pitcher. I didn't come in well on right-handed hitters. I wanted to throw the ball down and away. What made Elston tough for me was he had that closed stance and I didn't have enough juice to get it by him inside, so he would take it to right field where the fence was about four feet high and 344 feet away before they remodeled Yankee Stadium.

First Base: This is the one position I'm hung up on because in the American League most of the first basemen were left-handed hitters, like Norm Cash, Boog Powell, Jim Gentile, and later John Mayberry, and I didn't have a lot of trouble with them. A lot of them didn't play against me. In Detroit, for example, Cash wouldn't play and they'd play Jim Price, a backup catcher, against me.

Early on, Moose Skowron hit a home run off me, but I didn't face him that long, and I faced Dick Allen just a few times. So, I'd have to say the toughest were Tony Perez, who hit me pretty well, even though I didn't face him a lot, and George "Boomer" Scott. Boomer was tough in the midsixties, and he was part of that Red Sox team that won the pennant in 1967.

Second Base: Bobby Richardson. He retired in 1966, and they had a day for him in Yankee Stadium. I pitched that day. We got a bunch of runs early and I told Earl Battey, "If there's nobody on, tell Bobby we're going to throw him four or five fastballs; have a nice day."

He hit four of the easiest pop-ups. I told him I wish I knew that all those years when the winning run was on second and I pitched him low and away. He got as many clutch hits off me as Mantle and Howard did. He was a tough out, and he was also a good fielder. I faced other good second basemen, like Ryne Sandberg, for the short time I was in the National League, but I'll go with Richardson.

Shortstop: Luis Aparicio once paid me a nice compliment. Looie was a great bunter and he told Cesar Tovar that I was the only pitcher he wouldn't bunt against. I'll return the compliment. Aparicio, who could not only bunt and run but could hit and was a magician in the field, is my all-opponent shortstop.

Third Base: I share one record with Brooks Robinson, the third baseman on my all-time opponents team. We both have 16 Gold Gloves, the record. Brooksie's defense was so dazzling, people sometimes forget he had almost 3,000 hits, 268 home runs, and more than 1,300 runs batted in.

Outfield: I have four outfielders: one center fielder, Mickey Mantle, and one left fielder, Carl Yastrzemski. My two right fielders are Al Kaline and Frank Robinson.

When people ask me who the toughest hitter I ever faced was, Kaline is always the first name that comes to mind.

Frank Robinson came from Cincinnati and led the Orioles to the pennant in 1966. He doesn't get enough recognition. People always say Mantle, Mays, and Aaron when they talk about the great players of that generation, and Frank Robinson's name doesn't get added to that list enough for what he did. Not only did he hit 586 home runs, he was an outstanding all-around player.

I got Yastrzemski out pretty handily when I faced him in the minor leagues. The word on Yaz was even if you threw him soft stuff, all he did was flare it to left field. He didn't pull the ball. In Fenway Park, you could always pitch guys inside, try to get them to pull the ball, because they couldn't hit it out in right field. It was too deep. What you wanted to do was try to keep them from hitting it to left field. That's why they had all those left-handed batting champions—Ted Williams, Pete Runnels, Wade Boggs, Fred Lynn, Yaz. They'd keep their shoulder in and hit the ball to left field. In 1967, his triple crown year, Yaz started pulling the inside pitch, and he became a much tougher out.

That year, 1967, the Twins lost the pennant to the Red Sox by one game, and I blame myself. We were playing the Yankees in old Yankee Stadium, and I had a 1–0 lead, two out in the ninth, and Mickey Mantle batting, with Elston Howard on deck. When the count went to 3–1, manager Cal Ermer came to the mound and talked about walking Mantle. I told him I didn't want to walk Mickey with Howard coming up next. Besides, I had already struck Mantle out twice.

Boom! Mantle took it over the 457-foot sign to tie the game. The next thing you knew, a thunderstorm moved in and rained the game out. It was suspended after 10 innings, a 1–1 tie. I went back a month later and pitched the makeup game and got beat, 1–0. In two games, I gave up two runs and I got a loss and a tie. And we lost the pennant by one game.

That was the one time Mantle hurt me. As great as he was, I had a secret to pitching to him. He got me for 7 of his 536 home runs, and all 7 came with the bases empty. That was my secret: when you pitched to Mickey Mantle, make sure there was nobody on base.

CHAPTER **10**

No Game Today

I awoke with an empty feeling on the day after the Cardinals gave me my release. I had nothing to do. No job, nothing to look forward to. For the first time in 27 years, there was no ballpark to go to, no game to play. I was hurt by the way the Cardinals dumped me, and I was disappointed that I never heard from Whitey Herzog. He had gone off to Chicago to manage the National League squad in the All-Star Game, and he never called me. I thought after playing for so many years and knowing Whitey as well as I did, that I would have gotten a call from him saying, "Look, this is what we're going to do." Or even given me a chance to retire. I wouldn't have, but at least that would have taken the Cardinals off the hook.

It wasn't as if my ERA with the Cardinals was 8, or something like that. It was 3.89. They weren't using me a lot, but when I did pitch, I was still getting hitters out. It was as if Joe McDonald took delight in releasing me because we had some shouting matches on the phone over that contract dispute in 1982. I'm sure it was his idea and he influenced Herzog in this decision. It would never have happened with Chuck Tanner, who had been my manager in Chicago, but that was Whitey's other side. He could be tough.

The Cardinals came into Philadelphia in August, a month after the All-Star Game. I went to Veterans Stadium to see Bruce Sutter and John Stuper and some of my other teammates. I was standing on the field during batting practice, talking with some of my former teammates, when Herzog walked by and sheepishly said, "Oh, I'm sorry I didn't call you. We had to get to Chicago for the All-Star Game and the press conference." And that was it.

I was so hurt by what the Cardinals did, I almost made an issue of it, but the more I thought about it, the more I realized that after playing as long as I did, it would have sounded like sour grapes to complain. So I just swallowed hard and said that's the way it is.

A few days after I was released, I got a call from Tom Haller, general manager of the Giants. Mike Krukow was with San Francisco, and he and I had met through Sutter. Krukow had told Giants manager Frank Robinson that I could help them. So Haller called and said, "You can come in and finish the year."

I told him I needed some kind of guarantee for the spring of 1984 because I was getting paid for the rest of 1983, and to go to San Francisco without any promise for the future made no sense. If I wasn't going to pitch anymore, then I had to find something else to do. I passed on the Giants' offer.

For the last two and a half months of that season I kept getting up in the morning thinking, this is not right. What do I do? It was very frustrating.

That winter I was getting into broadcasting, and I went to baseball's winter meetings to do some radio work. At the meetings, I ran into Chuck Tanner and Harding "Pete" Peterson. Tanner was managing the Pirates. Peterson was their general manager. Chuck said, "You look like you can still pitch."

"I know I can still pitch," I told him.

They invited me to spring training and I accepted, so I was in the Pirates camp in the spring of 1984. They had Rod Scurry, Dave Tomlin, and a bunch of left-handed pitchers in camp. I knew I wasn't going to hook on with them, but Tanner said, "I'll spot you against teams that need left-handed pitching"—the Red Sox, for example. I'd face Wade Boggs, Jim Rice, Dwight Evans. I was 45 years old, and I was getting them all out. I had an agreement with the Pirates that on March 21 I would be free to contact other teams. I called Lou Gorman, general manager of the Red Sox, and said, "You can use a left-handed pitcher."

"You're 45 years old, Jim," Gorman said, "and we got this young kid, John Henry Johnson . . ."

"I'll make you a deal, Lou," I said. "If I'm on the disabled list, you don't have to pay me. You can put it in my contract. The only way I'll be on the disabled list is if my arm's broken. I *will not* be on the disabled list. I broke my wrist once, but I've never been on the disabled list in my career for an arm injury. John Henry Johnson is on the disabled list every year."

Gorman wouldn't go for it. About a month into the season, I was at home in Florida, my career apparently over. I picked up a newspaper and read the baseball news, and there it was. Disabled list, John Henry Johnson.

I had also talked to other clubs during the winter meetings. I talked to Sandy Alderson, general manager of the Oakland Athletics, and Dallas Green of the Cubs, but it was the same story. When you're 45, you're up against age and economics. They all fight this stuff about what kind of message they'd be sending to the young kids in their organization if they signed this guy who's 45. Today, I'd have a lawsuit for age discrimination. I probably should have pulled an "El Duque," Orlando Hernandez, and told them I was actually four years younger than the record book said I was.

Don't get me wrong. I didn't come into the game on a truck with a load of pumpkins. Working in Minnesota for Calvin Griffith, who was as penurious as they come, I'd known for years that it's a hard, cold business.

By winning 76 games over four consecutive seasons for the Twins, including 25 in 1966, I had reached the lofty salary (for the time and for a Griffith-owned team) of $60,000. In 1968, I was 14–12 and I took a cut. The next year I was 14–13. I took another cut. Then 14–10. Another cut. In 1971 I was 13–14. Another cut. I took a cut for four straight years.

I was determined to reverse the trend and get back to my 1968 salary of $60,000, so I worked hard to get myself in great shape for the 1972 season, and it paid off. I got off to my best start. I was 10–2 with a 2.07 earned run average when I broke my wrist and was out for the rest of the year. I wasn't sure how Calvin was going to treat me, but I found out when I got my 1973 contract in the mail. It was for the same money I made in 1972, $46,000. I told Calvin I wasn't going to sign it, that I had pitched well and was on my way to winning 20 games when I got hurt, and I wanted $60,000.

"I can't help it if you got hurt," Griffith said.

Calvin and I went at it pretty good. It got personal. Both of us refused to budge. I held out and refused to report to spring training. That spring, I was living just north of Orlando, where the Twins trained, and I worked out with the Rollins College baseball team.

Griffith kept sending his son, Clark, to my house, to get me to sign. They upped their offer to $51,000, then to $54,000, but I was adamant. I wanted $60,000. I agreed to report to camp without a contract and work out with the team. We flew to Oakland to open the season. On the day before the opener, Howard Fox, the Twins' traveling secretary, told me, "The boss wants to see you. He has your contract."

I went to Calvin's hotel room and he threw the contract on the table. It was for $60,000. I reminded him that there was a bonus clause in my previous contracts for winning the Gold Glove. He said, "You'd better sign that contract right now." So I did.

Calvin never even looked at me. He kept staring out this big picture window. We had had our differences in the past, but we always ended up shaking hands. This time when I signed my 1973 contract for $60,000, Calvin wouldn't even shake my hand. He just kept staring out the window. I told Phil Roof, my roommate, "I will not be with this team next year." And I wasn't.

Camilo Pascual won 20 games for the Twins in 1962 and 21 in 1963. When he got his 1964 contract, the raise was so minimal that he tore up the contract into little pieces, put it into an envelope, and mailed it back. Calvin had his secretary, Ruthie Stewart, tape it back together and send it back to Pascual. Eventually, Camilo got a modest increase. That's what it was like dealing with Calvin.

There were no agents in those days. We didn't have arbitration or free agency. I was Minnesota's best pitcher for 13 years, and 7 of my 13 contracts called for a cut. Every year I'd be fighting a cut, so Calvin and I would be at each other all the time. I can remember having talks with Harmon Killebrew, and he would say, "You should be a little nicer to Mr. Griffith. When your career is over, he might give you a job in the organization."

I said, "Harmon, when you quit hitting the ball over the wall, they won't know how to spell your name."

He found that out later. He was the Twins' greatest player, a Hall of Famer, but when his career ended, they offered him some menial job in the minor leagues. The Cardinals made Stan Musial a vice president, and the Twins gave Harmon Killebrew a job as their minor league hitting coach.

As far back as 1973, as I was approaching my midthirties, I began having thoughts about how much longer I was going to be able to play. In Minnesota, I had become friendly with Fred Cox, the place-kicker for the Vikings, and we used to talk about how when an athlete got into his midthirties and he didn't have a good year, it was easy to rationalize and say to yourself, "I've played 15 years and I've had a pretty good career." You fall back on that mentality. Fred and I were

---

I Can Go Home Again

For years I felt estranged from the Twins. After Calvin Griffith sold the team, many of the people who worked for him in the front office and around the stadium slowly died off or left the organization, and the new administration seemed to distance itself from the past. I had the feeling that the new Twins management had forgotten about those of us who had blazed the trail to Minnesota from Washington in 1961 and won the Twins first pennant in 1965. It was as if we were pieces of old furniture that you put up in the attic, out of sight.

Then, in 1998, I got word that I was being inducted into the Twins Hall of Fame and that I had been voted onto the Twins all-time team. When the Twins made the playoffs in 2002, I was invited to Minnesota, along with Bert Blyleven and Tony Oliva, to throw out the first ball in Game 1 of the ALCS against Anaheim. This was all the brainchild of Dave St. Peter, the Twins senior vice president for business affairs.

Going to Minnesota and participating in the pregame ceremonies was one of the most memorable and moving experiences of my life. The reception we got from the fans and the team was heartwarming. It was an experience I'll never forget.

Before the first-ball ceremony, they showed a 35 to 40 second video of each of us on the message board, highlighting our careers and promoting our credentials for the Hall of Fame.

Needless to say, I'm flattered when people say or write that I belong in the Hall of Fame. It's not false modesty when I say I don't think of myself as a Hall of Famer, which I believe should be reserved for the all-time greats. I consider myself an all-time survivor and an above-average performer, but not an all-time great.

Perhaps if I had won 300 games, I might have been elected to the Hall of Fame by now. But two injuries—a broken navicular bone in my wrist in 1972 and a lateral crack in my kneecap in 1976—may have cost me the 17 wins I needed to reach 300. I'm not looking for sympathy. I didn't play this game to get into the Hall of Fame. I played it because I had a passion for the game and a love to compete.

As much as I would love to be elected, I believe it would be a travesty if I ever got in before four more-deserving people: Marvin Miller, Curt Flood, Tony Oliva, and Bert Blyleven.

---

talking about how if you really enjoy playing and you want to keep playing, you have to condition yourself like you're a rookie going to spring training. From 1973 on, that's what I did. I went to Florida in mid-January and started throwing and working out, getting myself conditioned like I was a rookie trying to make the team.

I never set any goals for myself, either for longevity or with specific numbers in mind. When I got to St. Louis, I still had a chance to win 300 games, but when Herzog took over as manager, he told me I could be valuable pitching out of the bullpen. I knew I wouldn't get a chance to win many games in that role, but Whitey said, "You can help us win the World Series," which we did.

Some players have specific goals. Don Sutton made it clear he wanted to stick around long enough to win 300 games and pitch 60 shutouts, all the things that went along with automatic election to the Hall of Fame. He won his 300 games, 321 to be exact, and he fell two short of 60 shutouts. And he did get elected to the Hall of Fame. I can honestly say I never played with that in mind. I just enjoyed playing. I loved the game. I wanted to play as long as I could. Being left-handed, I found a role as a reliever that enabled me to play three or four additional years. The competition, the love of the game— that's what kept me going.

I can remember early in my career telling one of my first room- mates, Jack Kralick, "Baseball is a great game; I just don't know how much longer I can afford to play it." We'd be watching Whitey Ford warming up and I'd say, "Wow, he makes $50,000 a year. Can you imagine doing that for five years? You'd have enough money to retire."

When I was in Philadelphia, Steve Carlton and I used to have this saying, "We're never going to join the human race; we're going to pitch forever." There was a popular song at the time, something about "I'm going to live forever," and Dave La Point, who had been with me in St. Louis, would substitute the word *pitch* for the word *live*.

Young pitchers would look at me, and I knew they were think- ing, "They got this guy, he's 37 years old." I'd kid them. "You guys want to come to a game this summer, give me a call; I'll leave you some tickets."

It was a matter of pride that here I was 42, 43 years old, what- ever, and I was playing with guys young enough to be my sons, and I was able to compete with them.

When my career ended, I had played in the major leagues for 25 seasons, longer than any other player in the history of the game at the time. Tommy John passed me by a year, and Nolan Ryan passed

Tommy by a year, but when I left I had played the longest. I was very proud of that.

I didn't keep playing to set some kind of record or because I wanted to play longer than anybody else. I really enjoyed playing. Nobody goes into baseball thinking he's going to play 25 years in the major leagues. I certainly didn't. The average length of a major leaguer's career is less than four years. Just to make it to the majors is a long shot. For anyone to think he's going to be able to play for a quarter of a century is ridiculous.

CHAPTER **11**

A Rose Is a Rose
Is a Rose . . .

Thoroughbred racing is one of my favorite pastimes, and Saratoga is one of my favorite places. Whenever I'm free, I try to attend the annual meeting in Saratoga. In the summer of 1984, I was free. I had been out of baseball a year. I still felt disenfranchised, still floundering, still trying to figure out what direction I wanted to go. I was doing some college games for ESPN, but, frankly, the prospects of a career in broadcasting didn't seem very bright.

I was driving up to Saratoga with a trainer named Lofty Bruce whom I had met at the Meadowlands. We had the radio on and we heard, "Pete Rose named player/manager of the Cincinnati Reds." I said, "I'm going to get a call tomorrow."

My relationship with Rose began in 1976 when we competed against each other. I was with the Phillies, and he was with the Reds.

Pete had that barrel-chested run, head down, chest out. In Philadelphia, the visiting dugout is on the third-base side, and when Pete made an out, he would circle around first base on his way back to the dugout and run past the mound to intimidate the pitcher. I'd see him coming and, just to play games, I'd move into his path so that he had to make a choice: either run around me or run over me. He'd kind of give me a glance out of the corner of his eye, so there was that little competitive gamesmanship we had going on.

In 1979, Rose signed as a free agent with the Phillies, and we were teammates for about a month, until I got traded to the Yankees. A year later, I ended up with the Cardinals. We were playing against the Phillies one day, and Henry King, the Phillies batting practice pitcher, came over and said, "Pete wanted me to tell you that if he ever gets a managing job, he wants you to be his pitching coach."

I didn't remember talking a lot of baseball with Rose, and I wasn't particularly close to him, so I was taken aback somewhat. We were teammates for only a month, plus six weeks in spring training, and we competed against each other for three seasons. But I think he liked my approach to the game, and I thought, "Wow, that's pretty flattering."

Driving to Saratoga, I mentioned this to Lofty Bruce, and he said, "He's probably told that to 10 guys."

I said, "One thing about Pete, he's very loyal."

Sure enough, the next day, I called back to my farm in Pennsylvania and was told, "Pete Rose is trying to reach you." I tracked him down and he said, "I want you to come in and be my pitching coach."

The call was very timely. I was out of a job and getting restless. My broadcasting career was at a standstill. The thought of being a pitching coach intrigued me. Having had outstanding pitching coaches Johnny

Sain and Eddie Lopat, I always wondered what it would be like to coach pitchers. I had some ideas I was eager to try out.

After Pete called, a meeting was set up for me with the general manager of the Reds, Bob Howsam, to talk contract. In that laconic way of his, Howsam said, "Jim, Pete wants you to be his pitching coach, and you've never had any coaching experience."

"I know, Bob," I said. "I hope that pitching for 25 years has given me enough experience that I can be helpful to some pitchers."

He said, "We don't pay a lot of money to our coaches."

"I understand that," I said. "I'm doing this for one reason: I'm flattered that Pete asked me."

"We can pay you $45,000. That's all we pay our coaches."

It wasn't a lot of money, but I was curious to find out what kind of pitching coach I would be, if I could implement my theories and help some pitchers. I accepted, mainly because of Pete. I was not only flattered by his offer, I liked being around him. I liked his fire and intensity, his approach to the game. I appreciated the fact that under Pete, I would have free reign over the pitchers. When I eventually left the Reds, it was because of their frugal ways. I just wasn't making enough money to continue. It had nothing to do with Pete Rose. Working with him was a delight.

I always enjoyed Pete. I respected his competitiveness and his work ethic. As a player, Pete was driven. He was the type of guy who, if he got four hits in a game, he wanted five. And I appreciated his interest in the history of the game and the players who came before him.

One night in Philadelphia, Larry Bowa got a double and they put on the message board that that particular hit tied Johnny Callison for sixth place on the Phillies all-time list. Pete had nicknames for everybody. Mike Schmidt was "Herbie," and if you asked Pete why, he'd say, "He looks like a Herbie." Bowa was "PeeWee" because he's a little guy. So Bowa got his double that tied Johnny Callison, and Pete said, "PeeWee, you tied Johnny Callison. Wait, I'll put some real names up there for you."

A day or two later, Pete hit a double, and on the message board it said, "Pete Rose passed Ty Cobb and tied Stan Musial for third place for the most doubles on the all-time list," and Pete was standing on second base, pointing to the message board and shouting into our dugout at Bowa, "See, PeeWee. Those are some names."

The interesting thing about that for me was Pete's awareness of where he stood on the all-time doubles list and that he knew who was ahead of him on the list.

One of my great days in baseball was the night in 1985 that Rose broke Ty Cobb's hit record. The 30 days leading up to that were unbelievable. One night he went oh for four and said, "Kitty, tell the writers I'll be there in a little while." He took Billy DeMars, one of our coaches, and he went to the batting cage underneath the stands and took batting practice at 11:00 at night.

Pete was one hit away from the record, and we were in Chicago on a Sunday, a terrible, rainy day. Steve Trout was pitching for the Cubs, which meant Tony Perez was playing first base and Pete wasn't playing. The Cubs had a big lead and it started raining. We were in a rain delay, it looked like the game would be called off, and Pete wasn't in the lineup anyway, so the writers who had been following Pete, waiting for him to break the record, got up and left for the airport to fly to Cincinnati for the next game.

It stopped raining, the game continued, and we rallied. The Cubs brought in Lee Smith. Now we had a chance to win the game. Pete was standing next to me in the dugout. He looked in the stands; there couldn't have been three thousand people left, and all the writers were gone, and Pete said, "If we tie this game, I gotta hit."

He realized that if he did not put himself up to hit, he would have been second-guessed. People would have said that the record was more important to him than winning the game, and that wasn't the way it was with Pete. Winning was always more important to him.

I'm thinking, "Man, the writers have been following him around forever, and now he could get up there and hit a bloop single and break the record and nobody will be there to see it."

He did get up against Smith and drew a walk in an extra-inning game, so he still hadn't broken the record. We had the next day off, and then we started a series against San Diego on Tuesday night in Cincinnati. Pete went oh for four against Andy Hawkins. The next day, we were in the coaches' room and Pete came in and Tommy Helms said, "You know what, Scooter, last night was the first time in all the years I've known you, you didn't look like you were having any fun playing baseball. You always have fun playing baseball."

He was pressing so much to get that hit to break the record. That night, he got the hit against Eric Show in his first at-bat and he had the record.

There are a couple of players I played with, or against, who were legendary. Harmon Killebrew was one because of some of the home runs he hit. In Tiger Stadium one night, Harmon took Jim Bunning over the roof, one of the first times that ever happened. Dick Allen was another player who was legendary. And Pete was in that category. You'd look at that little squat body—he couldn't run very fast, he couldn't throw, but he could just play baseball. Nobody respected Pete more for what he did on the playing field than I did. You'd like to have a 40-acre field full of guys who played the game the way Pete played it. Whenever you'd talk to somebody about playing the game, his name would come up. They'd say, "That's the way the game should be played."

When I joined Rose in Cincinnati, I said, "You know, Pete, I have some definite opinions on pitching. I came up in the four-man rotation. Guys threw a lot."

He looked at me and, in his profane way, said, "Kitty, you know me, I know hittin'. I can bleepin' hit. But I don't know nothin' about pitchin'. You do whatever you want with the pitchin'."

That was fine with me. He even wanted me to make pitching changes, but I told Pete, "The one thing I don't feel comfortable doing is making pitching changes. If I go out to bring in a new pitcher and you're standing on first base and there's some doubt in your mind, that's not right. It's your job on the line. I'll make suggestions for you, but you should make the changes yourself." And that's the way we left it. It was a good working relationship because Pete would be playing and yet he was so aware of what everybody else was doing. He had that unique baseball mind that he could play first base and hit and know what he had to do to play the game, and at the same time, he would say, "How's Browning doing? They got Guerrero coming up next inning." It was amazing to me that he could be thinking about hitting off Doc Gooden and still have his head in the game as a manager.

I'm shocked nowadays when I hear a player say, "Who's pitching against us tonight?" The guy's in the lineup, and he doesn't even know who he's going to be hitting against. I can remember being around Pete and he'd say, "We're going to Pittsburgh next week and then the Dodgers and they're going to have Valenzuela, Hershiser, and Welch. Last time out, Valenzuela worked six innings. He ain't been pitchin' good lately. Can't get his curve over." He knew who we were playing, he knew the other team's pitching rotation, and he knew how they were pitching. He was amazing.

There were two things that Pete Rose and I had in common. One was our love for baseball, its history and tradition. The other was

110

thoroughbred racing. I love thoroughbred racing. I'm not a gambler, but I enjoy the sport of it. I don't mind putting down a couple of bucks here and there, but Pete was a big-time player. We'd go to the races and I'd bet my $20 to win and Pete would have a stack of tickets that, as the old saying goes, a show dog couldn't jump over. He was compulsive, obsessive about it. Many times on a day off or at night after a day game, we'd go to the races. I knew he was a big player, but I never thought it was any of my business how much he bet.

The first inkling I had that Rose was in any kind of financial trouble came when a couple of times after a game, I'd say to him, "Scooter"—Tommy Helms, who was a coach with us, gave him that nickname—"we going out for dinner tonight?" And Pete would say, "I've got an appearance tonight. I'm going to sign autographs."

That kind of raised my eyebrows. I thought that was strange because the guy was making plenty of money and I knew he liked his relaxing time. I figured he had to give a good chunk of what he made signing autographs to the government. I didn't see it as being a real profitable deal. Then the next day, he'd have huge amounts of cash that he got from these autograph shows. Later, when all that stuff came out that he had problems with the bookies, it dawned on me that he was trying to generate some cash to pay off the debts that he incurred.

I've heard all the rumors, the theories and opinions about Pete: that he bet on baseball, he bet on Reds games. I have theories of my own, but no evidence one way or another. I was long gone as the Reds' pitching coach when all his problems descended upon him and he was suspended from the game. I had made up my mind in the middle of my second season in Cincinnati, 1985, that I was not going to return the next year. The reason I left was purely economic.

I was putting in many more hours as a coach than I ever did as a player, with preparation, meetings, working with the pitchers on the

111

side, and the Instructional League. I told Pete, "I enjoy doing this, but if they could just make it somewhat worth my while, if I could get a three-year deal that would get me up near the $100,000 level, I'll stay."

But the Reds wouldn't budge. Just about that time, some broadcasting opportunities opened up and I told Pete that unless I could get three years at some decent money, I was going to pursue broadcasting because it was going to be much more lucrative and it was going to be an easier way of life. Pete understood. The one thing he could identify with was money.

When it came out in 1989 that Rose was getting suspended, one of the things that clicked with me was that he was said to be betting $2,000 a game. That was his standard bet on Sundays when he bet NFL games—$2,000. So that rang true to me.

At the time, I was doing some work for ESPN, and I was assigned to cover spring training. One of my stops was the Reds training camp in Plant City, Florida. Pete had not been suspended yet, but they were closing in on him. Rumors were strong that he was involved in gambling, and there was a horde of reporters in front of the Reds clubhouse.

I went around the side and found Bernie Stowe, the equipment manager, and I said, "Bernie, I've got to do an interview with Pete."

Rose came out the back door and we did a one-on-one interview. I said, "Pete, I've got to ask you, did you bet on baseball?"

He said, "No, I didn't."

Off camera, I said, "Be up front; be honest."

I was trying to convince him that no matter what he did, as we see now by looking back at Darryl Strawberry, Steve Howe, Doc Gooden, and countless other cases, the public will forgive you if you just come clean, admit what you did, and show some remorse. But he was adamant and always has been.

The evidence baseball had against him was overwhelming. Bart Giamatti was the commissioner at the time, and he had such a love and reverence for the game, you couldn't help believe that the information he had that never came out was enough to implicate Pete.

From what I witnessed when we were together as teammates and when I coached for him, a lot of things added up, and I'd have to say I believe he did bet on baseball. However, I don't think he bet on Reds games. I always believed that what made Pete a great player is that he thought he was bulletproof. He could do anything, and he could get by with anything. In this situation, I'm convinced that if he had come out and said, "I made a mistake," people would have forgiven him. We've come to understand that gambling is an addiction, like chemical abuse or alcohol abuse, but you have to admit it. And Pete never has admitted it.

Baseball has always been stringent when it comes to gambling. It's the one thing baseball cannot and will not forgive. It goes back to the Black Sox scandal, when eight members of the 1919 Chicago White Sox were accused of throwing the World Series to the Cincinnati Reds. Even though they were acquitted in a court of law, they were suspended from baseball for life and never reinstated. That's how frightened baseball is of the public perception that the game is not on the up-and-up. And that's why in every clubhouse in every professional stadium in the country, from the lowest minor league to the major leagues, there's a prominently placed sign as big as can be warning players that gambling on baseball will result in a lifetime suspension from the game.

You could be an ax murderer or a convicted rapist, and your chances of being absolved and reinstated by baseball would be better than if you were accused of betting on the game.

I learned about this firsthand when I was with the Chattanooga Lookouts in 1959. The Southern League had a lot of former major leaguers, old timers who were hanging on for a paycheck. I roomed with Ernie Oravetz, a little switch-hitting outfielder, and we'd walk into the park and there would be a group of guys and they'd yell, "Hey, Ernie, you going to foul the first pitch off? How about taking the first pitch?"

I was 20 years old; I didn't know what was going on. I asked Ernie. He said, "Look at that section above the third-base dugout. Half of the stadiums in this league, that's what our attendance is. These guys are betting on every pitch. Foul ball. Fair ball." The Southern League was a huge betting league. Guys would bet $5 that the first time a batter made contact, the ball would be fair or foul. Things like that.

Mobile had a player named Sammy "Buttermilk" Meeks who got traded to Chattanooga. The first thing he did was go to our owner, Joe Engel, and say, "You got something funny going on with your club." This was because when we played Mobile, Jesse Levan, our first baseman, told Sammy, "Look at our shortstop; he's giving away our pitches. He bends over on a curveball and he stands up on a fastball."

So Sammy told the Mobile hitter, "I got their pitches."

I was pitching a game against Mobile and Jesse fielded a ground ball with a runner on first and he fired it into left field, about 20 feet over the shortstop's head. I didn't think anything of it at the time. There were some bunts down the third-base line and Tommy "Buckshot" Brown, who played in the big leagues at the age of 16, started yelling, "Let it go, let it go." I looked at it and I said to myself, "That ball's not going foul. What's going on here?"

What was going on was a betting scandal. It all came to light when George Trautman, the commissioner of minor league baseball, had hearings to investigate the rumors of betting in the Southern League. They interviewed all of us about certain games we had lost. The governor of Tennessee even got involved. They had information that Jesse Levan was supposedly offered $500 a game to leak information to the gamblers; he was eventually banned from baseball for life. A few guys were thrown out and that's how I learned, at a young age, that the one thing baseball would not tolerate was even the hint of a betting scandal.

To this day, the question remains: should Pete Rose be allowed in the Hall of Fame? Obviously, it's a no-brainer that he belongs based on his playing record. But that's not the issue.

It broke my heart when I attended the Hall of Fame ceremonies when Richie Ashburn and Mike Schmidt were inducted and there was a large delegation from Philadelphia in attendance. As they were introducing the Hall of Famers—Johnny Bench, Joe Morgan, and the rest—fans were chanting, "We want Pete, We want Pete." And Johnny Bench got up on the podium and said, "You can have him."

Bench and Morgan, who were his teammates in Cincinnati, are both adamant about Pete not being admitted to the Hall of Fame because he didn't admit what he did. I tend to agree, unless he came clean and admitted his mistake. Now, I think it's too late.

I always thought there should be a way to recognize him for his accomplishments but at the same time not officially induct him. For example, have a Pete Rose exhibit or a plaque detailing his playing career and stating the reason he wasn't inducted. In other words, give him his due as a player, but make an example of him as a lesson to youngsters and a warning to other players. But, I'm afraid it will never happen.

CHAPTER 12

Throw Strikes . . . Work Fast . . . Stay Ahead . . .

I spent two years in Cincinnati as Pete Rose's pitching coach, and I enjoyed every minute of it. I would have continued, but it was no longer economically feasible. What I liked about it was that it gave me an opportunity to implement some of my theories of pitching, which I had formulated from two excellent pitching coaches, Johnny Sain and Eddie Lopat, and from my own experiences.

Sain won 20 games or more four times, including three years in succession, for the Boston Braves in the forties when they had the slogan, "Spahn and Sain and pray for rain."

Johnny's strength was showing you how to make the ball move and boosting your confidence. You might have a mediocre curveball and he'd make you believe it was as good as Koufax's. He preached that a pitcher has the advantage; he has the ball. Nobody knows what he's going to throw. Look at Sain's track record, at all the 20-game winners he coached: Whitey Ford, Mudcat Grant, me, Mickey Lolich, Dennis McLain, Stan Bahnsen, Wilbur Wood. Everywhere he went, pitchers improved. From Sain, I also learned what he called a short curve, which is somewhere between a slider and a curve. He called it a controlled breaking ball. If I had a hitter 3–0 and I was concerned about him having the hit sign, I had confidence that I could throw that pitch for a strike just about any time I wanted to.

Sain also taught me the slide step with men on base, which just about every pitcher uses today. I may have been the first one to do it. There was very little speed in the game in those days. Luis Aparicio with the White Sox was just about the only base stealer in the American League. Then the Oakland A's came along with Bert Campaneris, Billy North, and Herb Washington. Sain taught me to shorten my delivery. I was able to get the ball to the catcher in 0.9 seconds. Nowadays, if a pitcher gets it to the catcher in about 1.3 to 1.5 seconds, he's doing well. A good catcher's throw reaches second base in 2 seconds, so if I got it to the catcher in 0.9 to 1.1 seconds and the catcher threw it accurately, there wasn't a man alive who could steal second base.

Lopat was "Steady Eddie" of the Yankees, a 21-game winner in 1951 and a model for what has become known as the "crafty left-hander." He taught me to make my curve work *for* me, not against me. He convinced me the important things in pitching were movement, strike one, get ahead of the hitter. The advantage is always with the pitcher on 0–1. Eddie taught me how to change speeds on my curveball, to throw it at two or three different speeds.

Much of what I learned about pitching from Sain and Lopat I still apply today as I fight the ever-constant, unwinnable battle of trying to put a little white ball into a small hole in the ground. Legendary golf pro Bob Toski, who is helping me with my game, reminds me a great deal of Johnny and Eddie when he preaches about grip adjustment, touch and feel, and just plain common sense.

As a result of what I learned from Sain and Lopat, and what I picked up on my own, I brought my own pitching theories with me to Cincinnati. For example:

- I believe the fastball is still the best pitch in baseball because it's the only pitch you can throw to all four corners of the strike zone.

- I believe low and away is better than high and tight.

- I believe strike one is still the most important pitch.

- I don't believe a pitcher benefits a great deal from running.

In 1964 I had a little back strain and it hurt every time my heel hit the ground when I ran. So I told our pitching coach, Gordon Maltzberger, "Running these wind springs is not good on my back." His comment was, "OK, but you probably won't have much stamina in your next few starts because you won't have good legs." The next month I pitched four extra-inning complete games and my legs never felt better. I kept kidding Gordon, "How come my legs are feeling so great when I'm not running those wind sprints?" The lesson there, once again, is that you pitch yourself into shape; you don't run yourself into shape.

- I believe in throwing every day. The arm is a muscle, and you strengthen a muscle by using it. I go by the adage that it will rust out before it wears out.

- The best drill for finding your rhythm and your proper arm angle is to pile up 15 to 20 baseballs on the ground, then reach back and pick up one of the balls and do a "crow-hop" or quick step like you're an infielder throwing to first base.

Roger Clemens still does this as part of his warm-up routine. It's an exercise I learned from Warren Spahn in the early sixties. I would go to center field with a bag full of baseballs and pile them up on the ground. Then I would reach back and pick up a ball and throw a one-hopper in to second base. I also liked to practice this by fielding round balls at shortstop during batting practice. I would do this two days after I had pitched. I found that it stretched and strengthened my arm.

Some of these theories, such as throwing every day, might have been considered unorthodox by the baseball establishment.

Ray Miller, when he was a pitching coach, had T-shirts made up that said: "Throw strikes, change speeds, work fast." I didn't have a good change-up like some of today's pitchers do, but I changed speeds a lot. I was more of a "take a little off, put a little on" pitcher.

To summarize my philosophy of pitching: throw strikes, work fast, and stay ahead in the count.

Johnny Sain and Eddie Lopat both convinced me that as aggressive as you were in one inning, you had to be more aggressive in the next inning. There's a tendency for pitchers to get strike zone shy. I saw it happen to Hideki Irabu when he was with the Yankees. He was pitching against the Indians and, early in the game, he was throwing his fastball past the hitters. Then Matt Williams smoked one into the bullpen off his fastball, and Irabu's eyes got as big as basketballs. From that point, he wouldn't throw his fastball over the plate. Williams' bomb had scared him out of the strike zone.

In 1961, I had a 6–0 lead against Kansas City. Deron Johnson took me out of the park. Then Joe Pignatano hit one. Back-to-back home runs. I came right back to the next guy and threw strike one. I got him out, and I retired the side. When I got back to the dugout, Lopat said, "Now you're making progress. You gave up back-to-back home runs and you came right back with a strike."

Pitchers give hitters too much credit, and hitters do the same to pitchers. The old keep-it-simple philosophy still works. Fastball is the best pitch. Strike one is the best pitch. You don't have to be so concerned with throwing the ball on the corners early in the count. Movement is more important.

When I coached in Cincinnati, I took my pitchers out during batting practice and said, "Watch this coach. He's laying it in there and guys are popping it up, hitting it off the hands. They don't hit them all out of the ballpark. Throw strikes. Hitters are going to get themselves out if you give them the chance."

We've all seen home-run hitting contests. The hitter picks his own pitcher, tells him where he wants the ball, and still doesn't hit it out of the park. That's what I mean when I say pitchers give hitters too much credit. Hitters do the same thing. They overestimate what a pitcher can do. When Catfish Hunter was in his prime with Oakland, he'd get to 3–2 and get the hitter out, and that hitter would go back to the bench and say, "He just took a little off that pitch."

When I joined the Yankees, Catfish was there and we'd talk about that. It wasn't that he intentionally took something off the pitch, but on a 3–2 count, he needed a strike, so he probably didn't have quite as much on that pitch as he did earlier in the count. But it wasn't intentional. When the hitter said, "He just took a little off," he was giving the pitcher too much credit, like the pitcher was a brain surgeon.

One spring training when I was with the Twins, our pitching coach, Al Worthington, had Rod Carew, Harmon Killebrew, and Tony Oliva, all different style hitters, talk to the pitchers and tell them what they thought about when they were batting. Then Mudcat Grant and I talked to the hitters and told them our philosophy on pitching. I thought that was a great idea.

My Top 10 Pitchers

As far back as I can remember I have been a student of pitching—still am, because you never know it all. I used to hear from my dad about pitchers like his favorite, Lefty Grove, and others that he read about, like Cy Young, Walter Johnson, Grover Cleveland Alexander, and Christy Mathewson. I wish I had seen them.

In choosing my top 10 pitchers, I have excluded Bob Feller, Bob Lemon, Early Wynn, Warren Spahn, Robin Roberts, and other Hall of Famers because I either didn't see them pitch, saw them when I was too young to appreciate them, or didn't see them in their prime. I want to recognize these pitchers because I know what they accomplished, but I don't feel qualified to judge them. My list of top 10 pitchers dates back to 1960.

1. Sandy Koufax: He's on the top of my list, and for a four-year period, he may have been the best pitcher ever. From 1963 through 1966, he won 97 games, lost 27, struck out 1,228, and pitched 31 shutouts. He retired prematurely, at the age of 31, because of an arthritic left elbow. In his last season, he was 27–9 with a 1.73 ERA, 27 complete games, 317 strikeouts, and five shutouts.

Here was a guy who pitched for a team that didn't score a lot of runs, and he still was a dominant pitcher and a big winner. He had a great combination of power and control. Early in his career, Koufax had trouble throwing strikes. He became a great pitcher when he followed the advice of his catcher, Norm Sherry, and said, "I'm going to try to make the hitters hit the ball, not miss the ball." When he did throw free and easy and tried to make them hit the ball, they couldn't hit it because he had more movement on it.

2. Bob Gibson: He wasn't far behind Koufax. He had a great fastball, and a great slider, and he was maybe the best competitor I've ever seen for a pitcher. Also, he was a great all-around athlete who helped himself with his fielding ability and his hitting. Gibby hit 24 home runs in his career.

3. Juan Marichal: He's just a shade behind Koufax and Gibson in my book. That was a great era for pitchers, and Marichal was as good as anybody. He had an assortment of pitches that he threw from different angles, so it was as if he had anywhere from 12 to 14 different pitches.

4. Tom Seaver: He had a great fastball, a great slider, and 300 wins. They called him the "Franchise" when he pitched for the Mets. He was that, and more.

5. Steve Carlton: In 1972, when the Phillies won only 59 games, Lefty won 27 of them, an amazing 47 percent of his team's wins. He won more than 300 games and struck out more than 4,000 batters, second of all time.

6. Whitey Ford: I have a special place for Whitey, the "Chairman of the Board," because I won my first major league game pitching against him in 1960. In those days, the starting pitchers warmed up in the on-deck circles in Yankee Stadium, just to the left and right of home plate. One of my fond memories is warming up and looking over and seeing Whitey warming up on the first-base side. I was only 21, and I looked over and thought, "Man, here I am getting ready to pitch against Whitey Ford."

A year later, I hooked up with Ford again, this time in Minnesota, where the bullpens were side by side, separated by a chain-link fence. You were so close, you could practically reach across and shake hands with the guy you were pitching against. We're warming up and I could hear Whitey's fastball—". . . whirrrrrr . . ."—it had that spin on it.

There are two basic grips for the fastball, the two-seam grip and the four-seam, or cross-seam, grip. I had always thrown my fastball with the two-seam grip because the ball moved pretty well. I heard Ford throwing his fastball and I said, "Out of curiosity, how are you holding that pitch?"

He was very nice to me. He came over and showed me. It was halfway between the two-seamer and the four-seamer. It was sort of a side-angle, or off-center, grip. It just fit my hand perfectly. So I tried a couple and the ball went sinking down and away. I threw my fastball like that for 15 years, thanks to Whitey Ford.

7. Jim Palmer: He was in that era with Seaver, Carlton, Fergie Jenkins, and Catfish Hunter. You could choose any one of them and you wouldn't go wrong.

8. Ferguson Jenkins: He's still the only guy who has struck out more than 3,000 and walked fewer than 1,000. For a combination of power and control, he rates very high.

9. Roger Clemens: The Rocket would rate higher if not for the fact that, in today's game, pitchers rarely go the full nine innings. Today's pitchers leave in the seventh or eighth inning, and that has to detract from what they accomplish because the last six outs of a game are the toughest to get.

For that reason, I feel you have to put the Koufaxes, Gibsons, and Marichals in a higher category because they finished what they started. Take Sandy in the 1965 World Series, for example. He pitched a shutout on Monday and a shutout the following Thursday—two shutouts in a span of 72 hours against the most powerful hitting team in the American League.

I don't want to penalize Roger or Greg Maddux for not going nine innings. It's not their fault they don't pitch complete games. That's the way the game is played today. They're capable of doing it. In fact, early in their careers, before relief pitchers became as prominent as they are, these guys did pitch complete games.

10. Greg Maddux: He's similar to Clemens in that he's a victim of the current system. So, he'll pitch six, seven innings and then come out of the game because these days so much emphasis is on the bullpen.

I promised you my top 10 pitchers and I gave you 10, but the last two spots could easily go to any two of six special pitchers who are active today—Clemens, Maddux, Pedro Martinez, Randy Johnson, Curt Schilling, and Tom Glavine. In fact, I often change my opinion on which two of those six belong in the top 10. Let's just say you couldn't go wrong with any of them.

It was tough to leave off some outstanding pitchers like Nolan Ryan, Catfish Hunter, Phil Niekro, Don Sutton, Don Drysdale, Ron Guidry, Gaylord Perry, Jim Bunning, Bert Blyleven, Tommy John, and Jack Morris. They're all either Hall of Famers or close. Any manager would love to go to war with a pitching staff of the guys who don't make my top 10 list.

Today's pitchers have so much more going for them physically than we did in my day. They're bigger and stronger and they throw harder, but, with few exceptions, the feel for pitching isn't there. Pitching is more specialized today. Today's pitchers are into mechanics more than they are the touch and feel. Take Mike Mussina. He ran into a bad stretch because he'd get two strikes on a hitter and he'd try a little of this, a little of that, instead of going right at the hitter.

I said, "Mike, you can tell me to go jump in the lake if you want, it won't bother me, but I've been through what you're going through and I'd like to throw some ideas at you for what they're worth."

"Go ahead," he said.

"When I was having problems, I would walk down to Joe Adcock and say, 'Here it comes, Joe, a fastball right down the middle.' Or I'd start a game with the attitude, 'I'm going to throw batting practice today. See how far you can hit it.' You play mind games with yourself."

Mussina just looked at me like I was crazy. He went through Stanford in three and a half years; he can't think that simple. It's got to be more complicated than that for him. You can't imagine Mussina out there saying, "Here it is, hit it." He'll think, "How can I put on a little of this and a little of that." I knew when I left him he was shaking his head.

I saw Andy Pettitte when he came up. He could do so much more with the baseball at 22 than I could at that age. He had a fastball, good control of the curve, a change-up, and then he added the cutter, or cut fastball, which is a fastball that moves almost like a slider. I was basically a fastball pitcher. I threw a sinking fastball even to Mickey Mantle, who was a great fastball hitter. If I threw him a curve on the first pitch and it was ball one, he became a better fastball hitter. If I fell behind in the count, 2–0, I had no choice but to throw a fastball because I had to throw a strike. In that situation, Mantle was especially dangerous. But if I got ahead 0–1 or 0–2, I could throw a curve, and if I missed with it, I still had time to get him out with my pitch.

These days, a Pedro Martinez has four pitches he can throw for a strike at any time. The physical equipment is so much better today. The teaching aids are better. They have videotape and they grow up watching television and mimicking the major leaguers. They pick up stuff. We listened to games on the radio and looked at pictures in a magazine, and then we went out and tried to figure out how to do it.

You often hear it said about a pitcher, "He's got to pitch inside." It's one of the most overused sayings in baseball. In my opinion, you *throw* inside, but you *pitch* outside. In my day, the object of throwing inside was to keep guys from diving out over the plate. The idea of the brushback pitch was not to hit a batter but to keep him off the plate because you want to own the outside corner. You can't do that nowadays. They've taken the brushback pitch away from pitchers. So you see players like Derek Jeter who not only go out there for the outside pitch, they practically walk across the plate and fall all over themselves swinging at it. When I see that, my thought is if hitters did that in the sixties, their uniforms would be dirty all the time. I don't want to sound like I'm suggesting we were tougher, but the game was played differently back then. Today, it's almost like adult T-ball. Pitchers don't put fear in hitters any more.

In my day, the pitching philosophy was low and away, low and away. You never pitched inside early in the count because that's when the hitter is most aggressive and more apt to hit the inside pitch. Get two strikes on him, and a hitter will be more defensive. He'll protect the outside part of the plate. Then you can get inside on him.

Today, the philosophy is backward. They have better stuff today, but they don't read the bat as well. A low-and-away fastball with movement is still the best pitch in the game. That hasn't changed. But pitchers have a greater variety of pitches today, and they like to show them off. They'd be better off if they used fewer pitches.

Today's pitchers don't get the schooling we got. They don't spend a lot of time in the minor leagues, and even in the minors, they're on pitch counts. They rarely pitch when the game is on the line. Pitchers are out of the game in the late innings because they've reached their pitch count, so they haven't learned to pitch under pressure in game-winning situations.

Sain and Lopat both taught me to be my own relief pitcher. If, for example, I was facing Mantle and the first time he came to bat there was nobody on base, I wouldn't throw him every pitch in my repertoire. I might throw him one pitch and he'd pop it up. Maybe his third time up there would be two men on. Then I could go at him differently, with pitches he hadn't seen.

I see pitchers today use every pitch in their repertoire the first time through the batting order. Mussina again—in one game he threw 80 pitches in the first three and a fraction innings. I've had nine-inning games where I didn't throw 80 pitches. Mussina emptied the vault early so when it got to the latter part of the game he had nothing left and he was out of there. In today's game, with the relief specialists—the middle man and the closer—it's not necessary to save anything because most starting pitchers never see the seventh, eighth, or ninth innings.

You can't fault today's pitchers for not finishing what they start. That's how the game is played today. The game would be better if Roger Clemens and Pedro Martinez hooked up and pitched nine innings against each other. Instead, they're rarely around by the eighth or ninth inning. In 2001, Clemens became the only 20-game winner in baseball history without pitching a complete game. It's not that Clemens and Martinez are not capable of finishing what they start. They did it in the past. It's just that today's pitchers are not trained to go nine. The game has changed to the point where the philosophy is, "He's thrown 100 pitches and we're paying a closer $4 million to come in and get two guys out." Wouldn't it be a thrill to see Pedro with a one-run lead facing Derek Jeter, Jason Giambi, and Bernie Williams in the ninth inning?"

Let's say Clemens pitched eight shutout innings and was leading, 2–0, and then Joe Torre sent him out for the ninth with Mariano Rivera in the bullpen. If Clemens gave up two hits and Rivera came in and gave up a three-run homer, the second-guessers would be all over Torre. "You got Mariano down there making $9 million to save games; why didn't you bring him in?

I'm sure Torre and his pitching coach, Mel Stottlemyre, who go back to my era, cringe at it as much as I do when they remove a starting pitcher who has been effective in the eighth or ninth inning. I'm sure they would like to do it the way we did it in the sixties, but nobody does. There's no doubt in my mind that if they approached the game the way we did, Clemens, Martinez, Greg Maddux, Randy

Johnson, Curt Schilling, and all these great pitchers could pitch nine innings a lot more often than they do.

It would be fun to go to the ballpark to see Clemens pitching against Pedro knowing you had a good chance of seeing them pitch the full nine innings. My dad drove to Cleveland in the late forties to see a doubleheader between the Indians and the Yankees, with Bob Lemon and Bob Feller against Vic Raschi and Allie Reynolds, with eighty thousand people in old Municipal Stadium.

Johnny Sain used to say you never learn how to pitch until you hurt your arm. I hurt my shoulder and I broke a bone in my wrist on a tag play, and when I came back I had to make adjustments. Lopat and Sain taught me that you have to improve every year. To be as good as you were the previous year, you've got to be better.

When I got to Chicago, I had lost some movement on my fastball, and Sain wanted me to have a quicker release. I had a long, deliberate motion, but Sain thought I had lost some arm speed and suggested I shorten my motion. I tried it and John said, "No, you can still go faster than that." I told him, "OK, I'm going to pretend the bases are loaded and the batter just hit a one-hopper back to me, and I'm going to take it and throw it to the catcher like I'm trying to get a force play."

I did that and, using that fast motion, I won 20 games two years in a row. Brooks Robinson told me, "You picked up a little zip on your fastball." I said, "I really haven't, it's just that my motion is quicker." He said, "I don't have time to think about what's coming."

A hitter likes to get in the box and time his swing to the pitcher's motion. He likes time to think, "He got me out last time with a fastball . . ."

I wasn't giving them time to think about what was coming.

When Jerry Coleman was managing the Padres and I was with the Cardinals, he called a meeting and told his hitters, "I want you to step out and look for a sign on every pitch tonight. We're going to slow this guy down."

They stepped out of the box, but once they stepped back in, I was ready to go. They couldn't keep stepping out of the box forever.

I discovered that pitching quickly accomplished three things: it got me in a good rhythm, it didn't give the hitter time to think about what was coming, and it kept my fielders on their toes. When you see a guy walking around the mound, fussing and taking his time, it gives the impression he lacks confidence, and it causes fielders to relax and get back on their heels.

From not hitting because of the designated hitter rule in amateur ball, college ball, and the minor leagues, today's pitchers don't have a feel for how important it is for a hitter to have time to think when he's at bat. Throughout most of my career, there was no DH rule. I had to hit, so I know it's nice to be able to get in there, dig in, and get set. But if you've got a guy on the mound . . . here it comes, here it comes . . . you realize the effect that has on a hitter.

The first time I tried it was in the spring of 1975. On our way to Oakland to open the season, we stopped in Yuma, Arizona, to play an exhibition game against the Padres. I was facing Bobby Tolan. He got into the box and, zip, I threw him a fastball before he was set. He gave me a surprised look and I thought, "Man, this is going to work OK."

One time, there was a ground ball to third. Bill Melton fielded it and threw it to first base, they threw the ball around the infield, Melton threw the ball to me, and then he turned around to signal to the outfielders how many outs there were. When he turned around, the ball was being hit to him again.

I won 20 games in 1975 and pitched 10 games that were played in less than an hour and 40 minutes. In Anaheim, I was hooked up with Bill Singer. It was near the Fourth of July and the Angels were going to have a fireworks show after the game, so they moved the starting time up to 6:00 in order to start the fireworks at 9:00. We played the game in an hour and 35 minutes. The game was over, and we showered and dressed and were on the bus going back to the hotel, and they were keeping the fans in the stands until it got dark so they could start the fireworks.

In Chicago, if I was warming up to start a game, the vendors would shout at me, "Hey, slow down tonight." I was the least favorite pitcher of vendors, owners, and television producers. Once, when I was starting in Chicago, Roland Hemond said the television people wanted to know if I could take more time between innings.

"Do I have to do it?"

"No," he said.

"I want to get out there."

As soon as the last out was made, I already had my glove and I was running onto the field. I'd take about five warm-up pitches, they'd toss the ball around the infield, and we were ready to go. Some nights, we had two outs before they came back from a commercial break.

I wouldn't be able to pitch today. The television people would be on my back constantly, the owners would force me to slow down so they could get the commercials in, and the hitters, like Nomar Garciaparra, Chuck Knoblauch, and Derek Jeter, would keep stepping out to go through all their gyrations. It would drive me nuts.

Probably my most unorthodox theory is the one about throwing every day. Nobody does it anymore. I also learned that from Johnny Sain. I don't want to make this sound like the old "I had to walk 10 miles in a snowstorm" type of thing, but when we were kids, we shoveled snow, we mowed the grass, and we played every day; we did everything by hand so our bodies were somewhat developed by the time we were 18 or 19. And we just threw the ball every day. We played catch every day.

With the five-man rotation and pitch counts, pitchers don't get the chance to develop the arm strength they need.

When Stan Williams was traded to Minnesota from Cleveland in 1970, I pitched nine innings the day he arrived. The next day he saw me soft tossing in the bullpen.

"What are you doing?" he said. "You pitched nine innings yesterday. You shouldn't be throwing. You have to rest your arm today."

"No. I throw every day. I'm just exercising."

Ten years later, I was with the Yankees and Williams became my pitching coach. We were in spring training and Stanley was throwing batting practice every day.

"Steamer," I said, "how does your arm feel?"

"Better than it ever felt."

"See," I said. "You didn't throw enough during your playing career. If you had thrown more back then, you'd probably still be pitching."

Another of my unorthodox practices is that when I was coaching the Reds pitchers, I rarely went to the mound. I probably didn't go to the mound more than two or three times all year, and when I did it was to buy some time for a reliever to get ready, not to pass along advice. Joe Morgan was broadcasting Reds games, and if a pitcher was struggling, Joe would say to his partner, Marty Brennaman, "I would think the pitching coach would want to run out to the mound right now and talk to the pitcher."

The next time I saw Morgan I said, "Hey, Joe, you're hitting and the bases are loaded, you have a 3–2 count and the hitting coach calls time, calls you out of the box and says, 'What do you think you ought to look for, here?' How would you like it? You'd want to choke him, right?"

For years, position players have had this idea that pitchers are dummies, that everybody can tell them what to do. Fielders, who might not ever have pitched a game in their lives, are often going to the mound to offer advice to a pitcher. Turn the tables. How would Alfonso Soriano feel if he made an error and the pitcher ran over to second base and talked to him about his fielding? How would Mike Schmidt feel if he were hitting and I called time out and went to the plate and said, "I know this pitcher. He likes to throw a curveball in this situation"?

My Top Five Relief Pitchers

For the last five years of my career, I was mainly a relief pitcher, a role I came to enjoy a great deal. I liked starting games, too, because in my day managers would let you finish what you started. Johnny Sain always told me, "Be your own relief pitcher." By that he meant don't turn your game over to the bullpen; learn to complete what you start. One year, 1966, I started 41 games and completed 19, more than most *teams* finish today.

The one thing I didn't like about being a starting pitcher was waiting three days between starts (in my day, we pitched every fourth day, not every fifth day). I adapted easily to being a relief pitcher because it meant you had to be ready to pitch every day. That suited me fine. As I have said, I liked to pitch and I threw every day anyway, so I figured I might as well do my throwing in a game as in the bullpen or on the side.

In those five years, I came to appreciate the role of the relief pitcher, especially the "stopper" or "closer." I saw what relievers went through, coming into a game with the winning and losing on their shoulders.

Carrying that kind of pressure to the mound all the time is not easy. I compare short relievers to airline pilots and heart surgeons; people don't accept failure from them.

As a reliever, I also got to experience some of the crazy antics that go on in the bullpen.

Nowadays, if you pick up the phone in the dugout, it rings right through to the bullpen, but back in the seventies, you had to dial a three-digit extension to get the bullpen. They had the directory on the wall and you could use that telephone to call any place in the ballpark—either dugout, either bullpen, the front office—or to get an outside line. You can imagine the possibilities. We probably could have called China if we wanted to. Knowing some of the characters populating the bullpen in my day, I'm surprised nobody did.

In Detroit, the home team's bullpen was down the third-base line. It couldn't be seen from the Tigers' dugout, which was on the first-base side. The visiting bullpen was down the first-base line. You would get bored out there early in the game, especially in Detroit, where the bullpens were belowground, like a dungeon. The White Sox were in Detroit one day, and I was sitting in the bullpen. It was the fourth inning of a close game. Hank Aguirre was the Tigers closer, so I told our bullpen coach, "Let's call the Tigers bullpen and get Aguirre up."

I picked up the phone. A coach answered and I said, "Get Aguirre up."

Sure enough, Aguirre got up and started throwing. Their third-base coach looked down there and apparently mentioned to Mayo Smith, the Tigers manager, that Aguirre was throwing. They called down to the bullpen and sat him down.

Moe Drabowski once used the bullpen phone to order Chinese food sent to the ballpark. We would use the bullpen phone to make tee times. If it was an afternoon game and it was breezing right along, we'd pick up the telephone, dial "9" to get an outside line, and call out to the golf club. "We're in the eighth inning, we'll be out there in about an hour to get in a round of golf."

When I was a starting pitcher, I was warming up one day in Milwaukee, and Kenny Sanders, who had been my teammate and my golfing partner in Minnesota and who was now pitching for the Brewers, was watching me.

"You going out there with that trash and try to win?"

"That's all I got," I said.

Sanders had a great slider.

"Kenny," I said. "How do you hold your slider?"

He came over and showed me. He put his thumb on the side of the ball, which was unusual. Most pitchers put their thumb under the ball. I tried it and, wow, the ball really moved. I decided to use that grip to throw my slider in the game. It was the eighth inning and I had them shut out. I went to the phone, looked up the directory for the Milwaukee bullpen, and called down there and asked for Sanders. "Hey, Kenny," I said. "Thanks for the tip. I've been using that slider grip the whole game."

Probably more than any position in baseball, the role of the relief pitcher has changed dramatically over the past 20 or 30 years. In picking my top relief pitchers, it's tough for me to be objective because of those changes. There are a lot of guys who have 300 saves who I can't rate among my top five relievers—guys like Lee Smith, who's going to be in the Hall of Fame, and John Franco.

Today's closers, for the most part, will pitch one inning or maybe get one out and are credited with a save. Sometimes, the guy who really saves a game is the set-up man. He'll stop a rally in the seventh or eighth inning and then turn it over to the closer, who gets the save. Mariano Rivera is the best reliever in the game today. He may be the best ever. One day he came into a game with a three-run lead, faced the bottom third of the batting order, and got a save.

In the sixties and seventies, closers often pitched two innings or more, and they would usually come in with the game on the line and the tying run on base. Sparky Lyle doesn't make my list, but for a short time he was a dominant relief pitcher. In the 1977 American League Championship Series, Lyle pitched two and a third innings in

Game 3, came back the next day and pitched five and a third innings, and then came back the next day and pitched an inning and a third. Today's relievers aren't asked to do that.

Here, then, are my top five relievers.

1. Rollie Fingers: Like so many relief pitchers of that era, Fingers came up as a starter with Oakland, but he wasn't very successful. Harmon Killebrew, for example, could hit him blindfolded. Rollie made 8 starts in 1969, 19 in 1970, and 8 in 1971. His records were 6–7, 7–9, and 4–6.

In 1972, he was used exclusively out of the bullpen. Five years later, he led the National League in saves (for San Diego), at a time when if you saved more than 30 games, that was a lot. And he became the dominant closer in the game.

He was particularly tough against right-handed hitters because of his devastating slider. When Charlie Finley offered to pay $300 to any member of the A's who grew a mustache, Rollie grew that old-fashioned handlebar mustache that gave him an intimidating, menacing look.

He had great poise and exuded confidence on the mound. He could handle those pressure situations. When Rollie came into a game, he gave the impression that he was in control of the situation . . . and he was. And that was before the one-inning save. Often, he came in and pitched two innings or more for a save.

2. Bruce Sutter: I was with the Cardinals in 1981, and we were involved in a tight race in the National League East. We went to Shea Stadium for a big series with the Mets. We battled back from a four-run deficit and took a 6–5 lead into the bottom of the ninth. Sutter went in, so we figured game's over. He was that dominant. He got the first two guys out and Frank Taveras hit an 0–2 splitter, broke his bat, and hit a bloop single. Then Mookie Wilson took an 0–2 splitter over the fence and we lost the game, 7–6. It was a shocking loss.

Sutter called me "old timer" because I was the oldest guy on the team. He was the "Amishman" because he had that beard. Once we were on the plane going to Chicago and I said, "Well, Amishman, what are you going to do tonight?"

"I'm going to have a couple of cold beers and hope we have a one-run lead in the ninth inning tomorrow."

The next day, Joaquin Andujar pitched against the Cubs, and we had a 2–0 lead going into the eighth. Sutter pitched two innings and saved the game. He got right back on track.

What made Sutter so great was his demeanor and determination. He wouldn't get too high after he saved a game, and he wouldn't get too low on the rare occasions when he blew a save. He had the perfect temperament for a closer. And, of course, he was a pioneer in throwing the split-finger fastball, and his was devastating. For a five-year period from 1980 to 1984, the "Amishman" may have been the most dominant reliever of all time.

3. Goose Gossage: Goose had been a starter in the minor leagues, but he became an overpowering reliever, a dominant force with the Yankees in the seventies. He was another guy who would come in as early as the seventh inning to save a game.

I started a game against the Oakland A's during their championship run in the early seventies. I had a 2–1 lead going into the top of the ninth. There was a man on first, and they sent Billy Williams up to pinch hit. He got a ground single between first and second, and they had runners on first and third with one out. Here came Chuck Tanner to the mound, and I knew I was out of the game. The next two batters were Billy North and Bert Campaneris, two guys you couldn't strike out and you couldn't get to hit into a double play because of their speed. So I figured the best I was going to get out of that situation was a no-decision.

Gossage threw seven pitches. Campaneris tipped one. The other six were strikes. Goose just blew them both away, and I got the win.

In 1975, I started 41 games for the White Sox, and Wilbur Wood started 43. We were starting every four days and occasionally every three days. I had pitched on a Thursday night in Texas. I got beat, but it was a close game and I threw fewer than 100 pitches. We had a series with Oakland on the weekend, including a doubleheader. I was talking with manager Chuck Tanner and he said, "I told Gossage he would start on Sunday. I need another starter for the doubleheader."

"Chuck," I said. "I can start Sunday. I pitched Thursday, but I didn't throw a lot of pitches. If you start Goose and he pitches six innings, then you've lost him for four days."

Gossage, Bucky Dent, Terry Forster, and I all lived in the same apartment complex in South Chicago, and we would drive to the park together. Tanner had already told Gossage he was going to start, but when I convinced him to let me take the start, Chuck had to tell Goose he changed his mind. We were riding to the ballpark and Goose wasn't saying a word. I knew what was bothering him.

"You're hot because you're not starting Sunday, aren't you?" I said.

"Yeah," he said. "I was looking forward to starting."

"You're more valuable to us as a reliever. If you go out and pitch six innings and we don't win, we've lost you for four days. Right now you're a one-pitch pitcher. You're more valuable in the pen."

I started and, lo and behold, Gossage came in and saved the game.

The next year I was traded to the Phillies, and the White Sox made Gossage a starter. He was 9–17. The following year, Tanner became manager of the Pirates and he traded for Gossage and returned him to the bullpen. Once again, Goose became a dominant reliever, and I got to see him in the National League. The first time we played the Pirates, I called Goose over and said, "How did you like that starting?"

I can't talk about Gossage without coupling him with Terry Forster. They were a tremendous one-two punch in the bullpen for the White Sox—Forster a left-hander, Gossage a right-hander. In fact, Forster was considered the better of the two, and he might have made my top five list if he hadn't hurt his arm. As hard as Goose threw, Terry threw harder. Early in his career, when Forster was still a starter, he was pitching against Nolan Ryan in Anaheim. They had the radar gun on for Ryan and the fans could see the reading of the gun on the scoreboard. In the top of the first inning, Ryan was throwing and the sign showed he was hitting 97, 98 miles an hour, and the crowd was "oohing" and "aahing."

Then in the bottom of the inning, Forster went out and was hitting 100.

4. Dennis Eckersley: Eck is the only pitcher to have won 100 games and pitched 100 complete games as a starter and to have also saved 100 games as a reliever. John Smoltz, if he keeps doing what he's doing now and if he continues as a reliever, can be the next Eckersley.

5. Mariano Rivera: A lot of people believe Rivera is the best reliever ever. I'm not putting him down by picking him fifth, but he operates under a different system. I don't doubt that if he pitched in my era, he would have been just as dominant as he is today. It's not his fault he comes into a game only in the ninth inning, but I still can't rate him higher than Fingers, Sutter, Goose, and Eck.

CHAPTER **13**

"Boss George"

A year or two after I was out of baseball, I picked up the issue of *Sports Illustrated* devoted to the opening of the baseball season. I couldn't believe it when, on the cover, was a picture of George Steinbrenner wearing a Napoleon hat. That burned me. I fired off a letter to the editor accusing the magazine of poor taste. I pointed out that this was their baseball issue and instead of honoring one of the stars of the game—Mike Schmidt, Andre Dawson, Jim Rice, Cal Ripken, Eddie Murray, somebody like that— they put on the cover an owner who had been suspended by baseball, a man who stands for everything that's not good about the game. The magazine printed my letter in its entirety.

A short time later, *The New York Times* printed a letter from Steinbrenner's buddy, Bill Fugazy, defending George and portraying him as a charitable man. Fugazy listed all the good things George had done, all the organizations he had helped. I cut out the article and included it in a letter to Steinbrenner saying that because he was such

141

a charitable man, if it ever crossed his mind, he might consider sending me the $18,000 he owed me. I never heard from him.

When I left my job as pitching coach of the Cincinnati Reds after the 1985 season, I told Pete Rose I was going to try to get into broadcasting. Some people at an agency told me they thought I had a future in broadcasting and they wanted to represent me. I came to New York and started knocking on doors, looking for a job. One day, I picked up a newspaper and read an article about the Yankees revamping their broadcasting team. Jay Johnstone's name was mentioned and Bobby Murcer's. To my surprise, my name also was mentioned.

I called my agency. "I guess you're talking to the Yankees." They said they weren't.

I called the Yankees public relations department, a friend named Joe D'Ambrosio, and he suggested I call Don Carney of WPIX, Channel 11.

"I've been trying to reach you," Carney said. "We think you'd do well in this business. We want to hire you."

Carney asked me to come to WPIX to meet Leavitt Pope, who ran the station. They wanted me to be part of the Yankees broadcasting team. All they had to do was get George Steinbrenner to approve it. I told them that could be a major stumbling block. After the way Steinbrenner and I had bumped heads, I figured there was no way he'd approve me.

A few days later, Carney called to say Steinbrenner had no problem with WPIX hiring me. That's George; he'll let bygones be bygones and doesn't hold grudges.

I joined the Yankees broadcasting team in 1986 and worked with Phil Rizzuto and Bill White. Bill gave me one important piece of advice.

I Could Have Managed

From time to time, I have been asked if I ever wanted to manage. The answer is that I would have liked to give it a try, but only if my career had ended when I was in my thirties and I could have gone to the minor leagues to learn to manage, the way Tom Kelly did. Kelly is a man I have a lot of respect for as a manager. He played only 49 games in the major leagues, with the Twins in 1975, and he came up the ladder as a manager through the minor leagues. By the time he reached the major leagues, he was ready. He had handled all the situations a manager has to deal with on the field and off. I would have wanted to do it that way. I believe you have to go to the minor leagues to manage, just as you have to go to the minor leagues to learn to pitch. There are decisions you have to make as a manager that you never had to make as a player.

Some managers, like Joe Torre and Lou Piniella, never managed in the minor leagues and became good major league managers. They're the exception, not the rule. I didn't think it was possible for me, and, at my age, I didn't want to go down to the minors and start all over. I don't think I would have had any problem dealing with today's players, but there's so much more to managing than just dealing with players.

My time for managing has passed me by, so I'll just stay in the broadcast booth and critique other managers. It's a lot less pressure up there.

"Don't compromise your convictions," he said. "Talk about what you see. Just do the game. They're going to shoot a lot of messages to you. George might have a complaint about the umpires, and they'll try to get you to take up his fight. Don't do it. You'll probably last only one year, anyway, because that's the way it is around here."

Toward the end of the season, the people at WPIX said they were happy with my work and wanted to sign me to a multiyear deal.

They'd be in touch with my agent during the off-season. I kept calling my agency, and they gave me the run-around. I asked about the WPIX deal, and they said they hadn't heard anything. I knew something was up.

Bill White was right. After one year, George wanted to make a change. He had Billy Martin under contract, and Billy was doing some television. I didn't have a Yankee history, and I wasn't a cheerleader, so I was odd man out.

I found out later that an incident during the season had something to do with my getting let go. The San Diego Padres had banned beer in the clubhouse, and Goose Gossage, who was pitching for the Padres, spoke out against the team. The subject came up on the air during a Yankees game, and Rizzuto got on Goose for popping off.

"How can he say something like that? He's got to respect the authority of the ballclub."

"Well, Scooter," I said. "The first amendment. There's always been beer in the clubhouse. Goose was just speaking his mind, which is his right."

Apparently, Steinbrenner was listening that night, and he used that as an excuse to get rid of me.

I hooked up in Minnesota doing Twins games, and I did some work for CBS on the *Game of the Week*. Later, I was hired by ESPN. I was working for ESPN in 1994, the strike year, and I was Rollerblading down the streets of Madison, Connecticut, when I heard somebody call my name. It was Brian Burns, director of broadcasting for Major League Baseball. He said Madison Square Garden (MSG) Network, which carried the Yankees on television, wanted to hire me. Tony Kubek was retiring, and when he was asked if he had a suggestion on who should replace him, he graciously recommended me.

After 14 seasons with the Senators/Twins, I became a member of the Chicago White Sox. This photo is from 1975.

I won my only World Series ring with the Cardinals in 1982, my 24th major league season.

Pitching in Game 5 of the 1965 World Series. I spent more than half of my career with the Twins, but our parting wasn't very pleasant. The player on the left is shortstop Zoilo Versalles, the 1965 American League MVP. Photo courtesy of Bettman/CORBIS.

It was while I was with the Phillies that I formed a relationship with Pete Rose, which led to him asking me to be his pitching coach in Cincinnati. This photo was taken in 1978. Photo courtesy of Bettman/CORBIS.

Tim McCarver was a great teammate in St. Louis and has been a loyal friend and supporter for more than 25 years.

More than 35 years after I had the thrill of pitching to him in my rookie season, I had the opportunity to visit the great Ted Williams at his home in the Florida Keys.

I was invited to Cooperstown in 1995 for the induction of two great friends, Richie Ashburn (center) and Steve "Lefty" Carlton (right).

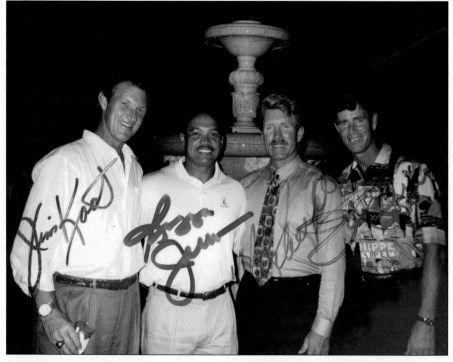

I was in pretty good company at Cooperstown in 1995 with Hall of Famers Reggie Jackson (second from left), Mike Schmidt (third from left), and Jim "Cakes" Palmer (right).

I'm proud to share one record with my friend Brooks Robinson—the most Gold Gloves, 16.

I was honored when the Twins invited me, along with Bert Blyleven and Tony Oliva, to throw out the ceremonial first pitch before Game 1 of the 2002 American League Championship Series. Photo courtesy of AP/Wide World Photos.

Bill White broke me in as a Yankee announcer in 1986 and has been a great friend ever since.

As talented a player as I've ever played with, Dick Allen did things that were legendary. I've cherished our friendship over the years.

I wasn't very happy with my job at ESPN. They're great people to work for, but they had me in the studio and I missed being in the ballpark. I called MSG and was told, yes, they wanted me to be part of the Yankees broadcasting team. But first . . . you guessed it . . . they had to talk to Steinbrenner. I said, "I think you're going to have a problem there."

I was home in Florida on the day before Christmas, on my way to play golf, when the telephone rang. My wife answered. "George Steinbrenner is on the phone," she said.

"Get out of here," I said. "I'm going out to hit golf balls."

"No, it's him."

I didn't believe it. I thought somebody was pulling my leg, but I took the phone and, sure enough, it was the Boss himself.

"MSG wants to hire you. You and I have had words in the past. I had a horrible relationship with Kubek. We didn't even speak. I don't want a relationship like that."

"George," I said, "whatever happened between us is past. I'd be there to cover your ballclub. I'm not going to use the game to talk about the disagreements we had." That was that. MSG hired me, and I've been a Yankees broadcaster since 1995.

CHAPTER **14**

On the Air

When you make the transition from player to broad-caster, the first thing people wonder is whether you're going to be able to criticize players. I never thought that was the right approach. The reason you get into broadcasting, at least for me, is not to criticize players. It's because you still have a passion for the game, you know something about the game, and you feel like you can communicate that knowledge.

A broadcaster's main job is to be honest and objective and right. If in doing that criticism comes into play, you have to stand up to whatever comes your way. If you're honest, objective, and fair, most players will accept criticism. Consequently, I have had very few complaints from players about what I have said on the air.

I have been fortunate to work with good partners. I learned a lot from Dick Enberg and later from Dick Stockton. One day Joe Garagiola gave me a little advice. I got broadcasting tips from Jack Buck. Tim McCarver and I were teammates, and we often talked about the broadcast business. He got into it before I did, and he has been very helpful and supportive.

I actually got started in broadcasting early in my playing career. In 1964 I did a postgame interview with Twins announcers Merle Harmon and Ray Scott. During the interview I was asked if I had any plans after baseball. I was only 25. I had no plans after baseball—just baseball. But I said, "What you guys are doing seems like fun."

A few days later, I got a call from Bob Zellner, the owner/manager of KSMM, a 5,000-watt radio station in Shakopee, Minnesota. He offered me an off-season job with the station and I launched my broadcast career as a jack-of-all-trades. I signed on at 6:00 A.M. with the national anthem, did news and weather, spun records, did play-by-play of local high school football and basketball games, and hosted studio talk shows.

I asked Harmon and Scott to critique my shows. They offered some valuable suggestions. I was horrible, but I learned a lot and the experience I got from working for that small radio station would come in handy in the future.

In my first game of my first tour of duty as a broadcaster for the Yankees, the Yankees had a three-run lead, two men on base, and Dave Winfield, the cleanup hitter, batting against Dan Quisenberry. Winfield attempted to bunt.

"Wow, that's really surprising," I said instinctively. "You don't see a cleanup hitter bunt, especially a guy like Dave Winfield. That shocks me."

I didn't rip him, but the next day in the paper, the columnist Dick Young mentioned what I said. In a way, he was complimenting me that on my first day on the job, I wasn't afraid to take Winfield to task.

I made it a point to go right into the Yankees clubhouse. I looked at Winfield, he looked at me, and he said, "I heard about it. It's no big deal."

Winfield knew I wasn't criticizing him, so it didn't become an issue. The important thing there is that I went into the clubhouse and gave Winfield the opportunity to confront me if he thought I was being critical of him. I believe that when you say something about a player that he might not like, it's important to be visible, to not duck the issue. Give the player a chance to vent if he thinks he has cause to do so. I know as a player that if you disagree with a writer or a broadcaster, and you want to discuss it with him, you appreciate it when that writer or broadcaster makes himself available, that he doesn't run and hide. I go into both the home team and visiting team clubhouses every day, and I hang around the batting cage, so if a player has a gripe, I'm right there for him to air it.

I once said something about Jim Leyritz that he didn't like. It was 1996, when we had a quote book on our telecasts. We would pick up a quote out of the newspaper from a player, one that was interesting or controversial, and flash it on the television screen. The Yankees had just acquired Charlie Hayes, and Leyritz was quoted saying, "I don't know why they got Charlie Hayes. Wade Boggs and I can take care of third base just fine."

I said, "If Jim Leyritz thinks he can play third base with Charlie Hayes, he hasn't seen Charlie Hayes play."

The next day Leyritz called me over. "My dad watches all the games," he said. "You ripped me on the air last night."

"I did? What did I say?"

He kind of shrugged. I told him exactly what I said. "If you want to go back and look at the tape, that's fine."

He backed off.

At about the same time, when Boggs was asked about the Yankees getting Hayes, he said, "I guess I'll have to go someplace else to get my 3,000 hits."

I said that when you're trying to win a pennant, that's a selfish statement to make. "Wade Boggs is a great player, he's going to the Hall of Fame," I said. "But right now Charlie Hayes is a better third baseman."

The next day, Boggs came to me and said, "I heard what you said. I didn't mean it to come out the way it did."

I'm sure I'm like every other player-turned-broadcaster. The players are in their lounge watching the games, and they might not like what I say. But I've never had any issues, and I've never had a player get in my face for something I said on the air.

I cover the Yankees. The YES Network, which is owned by George Steinbrenner, pays me, but I work for the viewer. I owe it to the viewer to tell what's going on in the game. I'm not supposed to suppress the facts, or distort them.

One time, when I was broadcasting Twins games, they were playing the Oakland A's. Jose Canseco and Rickey Henderson were both injured, and the team was winning without them. I made the comment over the air that Tony LaRussa was going to have a tough decision to make when Henderson and Canseco came back because Oakland was playing better without them. I walked into the A's clubhouse, and Rickey said, "Hey, that's the guy who said we're better with me and Canseco on the bench."

I said, "Well, Rickey, check the record." That was the end of that.

I'm fortunate to be doing Yankees games at a time when they're winning every year. I've broadcast for teams that were losers. It's no fun. I feel bad for someone like Byrum Saam, a great broadcaster who did Phillies games for all those years when they were losing and finishing last almost every year. That's got to be a tough job.

One thing that helped me is that when I started broadcasting, I did college games for ESPN. I had no affiliation. I was just there to do a baseball game, to talk about the players on both teams.

When the Yankees didn't renew my contract after 1986, I interviewed for the Cubs broadcasting job, and they asked me if I had a problem rooting for the home team. I said I couldn't do that in good conscience. There are people tuning in who may not root for the Cubs and are just baseball fans. I'm sure there are people watching Yankees games that hate the Yankees. You have to approach a game like you're not associated with the team.

At the same time, the advantage of covering the Yankees is that every day there's an urgency to win. Every day there are stories, like David Wells getting into a fight in a diner or Jorge Posada and El Duque pushing each other around in the clubhouse.

Let's be honest. In a perfect world, even though there are guys on other teams I like and would like to see do well, if the Yankees went 162–0, it would make my job easier. I see what goes on with teams that are losing, and it's not much fun.

People around New York have been very complimentary of my work. It's been flattering to hear their comments. But I'm not naïve. If the Yankees were 30 games out of first place, I would be criticized. If the team you cover is winning, you're part of their success. If they're losing, you become part of the losing, too. It's the nature of the business.

It's also human nature to form relationships and have favorites among the players. I like the games David Wells pitches because I like his approach. He's very simple, and the game flows along, so it's easier to do. Wells is a character who obviously enjoys what he's doing and where he's doing it, and that becomes infectious.

Mike Mussina is another story. He's as aloof a player on a team I'm working for as I've ever covered. Sometimes I'll go to Mike, ask him a question, and get a straight answer. Other times, he ignores me. And I've been a big booster of his. I thought he deserved the Cy Young Award in 2001. He pitched better than anybody else in the league, and I said so on the air.

Mussina pitched a game against the Red Sox in a rainstorm, and I noticed from his body language and his facial expressions that he wasn't happy. I commented, "If you take the mound on days like this with the thought, 'Why am I here? It's raining. We shouldn't be playing,' you're going to get beat every time. You have to understand that the elements are the same for both sides."

After that, when I walked into the clubhouse, he wouldn't even look at me. We don't have an acrimonious relationship. He's just aloof. It's not as enjoyable covering a guy like that as it was covering someone like Kirby Puckett.

Andy Pettitte is a player I like covering. He reminds me of me when I was his age, but he's more advanced than I was at that age.

There are players on other teams I enjoy watching. Ichiro in Seattle for one. I mentioned on the air how much I like watching Paul Konerko hit. When Ellis Burks first came up, I used to kid him. Whenever I'd see him I'd say, "My favorite player." I just liked the way he played. It was very enjoyable for me when Robin Ventura came to the Yankees. I first met Robin when I was doing college games and he had a 58-game hitting streak with Oklahoma State. Even Mussina. I saw him pitch when he was a freshman in college. I said over the air that he looked like he was ready to pitch in the big leagues right then, as a freshman.

Another nice thing about my job is that I run into a lot of former teammates and opponents who are broadcasting baseball for other teams or who just show up at the ballpark, which gives me a chance to renew acquaintances or catch up with old friends. Yogi Berra, Whitey Ford, and Reggie Jackson are around Yankee Stadium a lot. I mentioned that when we were teammates, it wasn't always pleasant being around Reggie. That's changed. Now I enjoy being around Reggie, who has become something of an elder statesman of the game. We have good conversations about baseball. He seems to have mellowed, and he's secure now with his position in life and his position in the game.

I was flattered that when the Yankees honored him on Old Timers' Day in 2002, Reggie asked me to attend. Hank Aaron, Willie Mays, and Ernie Banks were going to be there, and he kiddingly told me, "When you meet these guys, don't tell them how tough you were on me."

I could never imagine the Reggie Jackson who was my teammate saying something like that.

There was a time when I thought I wouldn't want to do this for too many years. When I was broadcasting in Minnesota, I started getting restless because the games were too long. A normal nine-inning game used to be two hours and 10 minutes, two hours and 15 minutes. They started to run two hours and 45 minutes and occasionally they would go three hours. I couldn't imagine a nine-inning game taking three hours. It took me a while, but I learned to build that into my thinking. Today, you have to figure on a game taking at least three hours.

That's one of baseball's problems. I hear people say, "I don't go anymore; the game's too long."

I don't care if the game is 10–1 or 1–1, at Yankee Stadium, by 9:30 people are going home. If there were forty thousand in the stadium when the game started, by 9:30 at least twenty thousand have left. That bothers me, but I don't want to keep using this as a platform to talk about what's wrong with the game.

Not every game is exciting. At times like those, the challenge for me is to make the broadcast interesting even if the game is dull and slow moving. If people weren't interested, they'd click off. I figure if there are people watching, they're watching for a reason. You have to try to give them something.

I have no intention of leaving this job anytime soon. I'm having too much fun. I still like the game within the lines. I like the pitcher versus hitter battle, and I like to see good players. And I'm with a winning team.

In the 13 years from 1982 to 1994, the Yankees finished first once (1994, the strike year), second three times, and third twice. That means that in the seven other years, they finished fourth or lower. In the eight years since I returned in 1995 for my second tour with the Yankees broadcast team, they have finished first six times and second twice, won five American League pennants and four world championships. I like to think there's a connection there, but there isn't. However, I have enjoyed their success. And I have benefited from it.

Lately, I have been reenergized working with our production team at YES. We have a great crew. It's like a baseball team. I enjoy working with them and being around them. I cover the best team and the best franchise. I get to make my own schedule. The way I look at it, I've got the best job in sports broadcasting.

CHAPTER **15**

On Second Thought . . .

I have changed my opinion of George Steinbrenner. I was so bitter about the treatment I got from the Yankees as a player that it colored my thinking about him and I accused him of being bad for baseball. When I see what's happening in baseball today, with this big-market, small-market situation, revenue sharing and the luxury tax, I have a greater appreciation for George's approach to winning.

I know what you're thinking. He works for the guy, so he's going to defend him and cozy up to him by saying nice things about him.

It's true that I cover his team, but you have to take my word that I haven't let that influence me. I'm sure there are times he's not happy with what I say on the air, and I don't always agree with his approach to things, but he's never said anything about it to me. We haven't had any problems since I returned to the Yankees broadcasting team.

155

I try to be objective. I try not to be a mouthpiece for the Yankees. I'll criticize them if I think it's warranted, praise them if they deserve praise. I think I have achieved that objectivity. At least, I hope I have.

George and I don't hang out. We don't socialize. We don't do lunch. But I haven't had any difficulty with him. I don't see him very often, maybe four or five times a year. He found out I enjoy thoroughbred racing, and he owns horses, so that's been our common denominator. When I see him, we're more likely to talk about horses than about baseball.

Since I returned in 1995, the Yankees have been very successful. They are the model franchise for baseball, so it's difficult to be critical of them. There's no reason other owners couldn't also have successful franchises if they were committed to winning like George is.

George can be a tyrant. He rants and raves, he can mistreat people from time to time, and he's very demanding, but when you see how many players want to play in New York now, you realize how he has transformed the image of the Yankees. That wasn't always the case. Not very long ago, players didn't want to come to New York because of Steinbrenner's reputation as an owner you wouldn't want to play for. Greg Maddux refused to come to New York. Even Roger Clemens, the first time he became a free agent, wanted no part of New York. Players used the Yankees just to drive up their price. Now that George has put together a successful organization with Joe Torre as manager, Brian Cashman as general manager, Jean Afterman, Gene Michael, and an excellent scouting and minor league department, and good baseball people like Billy Connors, Mark Newman, Gordon Blakeley, and Lin Garrett, it's become an attractive place to play.

Not only does George want to win, he's also big on Yankees tradition and history. He emphasizes tradition by making sure old

156

Yankees greats, like Phil Rizzuto, Yogi Berra, Whitey Ford, and Reggie Jackson, are involved with the team. The Yankees are the only team that still has an annual Old Timers' Day and the only team with an active alumni association. In 1973, George's first year as owner, the Yankees attendance was 1.2 million. It passed 3 million in 1999 and has been more than 3 million every year since.

When Steinbrenner bought the team, it was a depressed franchise. He paid $10 million for them in 1973, built up the brand, and once more made it something special to play for the Yankees. What would the franchise be worth now on the open market? $700 million? $800 million? $1 billion?

As bitter as I was in the late seventies and early eighties, now I look at how the Yankees operate and wish other teams would be as committed to winning. The Tampa Bay Devil Rays are a classic example. Small-market teams are clamoring for revenue sharing, yet Tampa Bay spends $13 million on Juan Guzman, $30 million on Wilson Alvarez, $8 million a year on Greg Vaughn. They've got John Flaherty, who's a nice guy and a decent catcher, but $3 million or $4 million for a backup catcher is exorbitant and not money well spent.

Nobody put a gun to the head of Tom Hicks, the owner of the Texas Rangers, and told him he had to give Alex Rodriguez $25 million a year when A-Rod's highest offer on the table was $13 million.

Forty years ago, when I was doing radio in the off-season, I had the opportunity to interview Bill Veeck, who was making a speech at Augustana College in the Twin Cities of Minneapolis and St. Paul. Veeck said, "What will kill baseball is the high cost of mediocrity." In other words, it's not the money you pay for the superstars that hurts you, but the ridiculous salaries teams are paying for mediocre players.

It's the owners' own fault. They throw money around wildly, make bad judgments. Meanwhile, Steinbrenner, with good people helping him make good decisions, spends his money wisely. Even with all his warts and flaws, George would win with some of these other franchises.

I think of Cleveland, because George came from there. It has often occurred to me how baseball might have changed if he bought the Indians instead of the Yankees. This may sound like I'm shilling, but I honestly believe that if he had owned the Indians during the nineties, they would have won at least one World Series, maybe more. Steinbrenner would have gone to John Hart, the general manager, and said, "What do we need? Do we need another pitcher?"

And, because of his insatiable desire to win, George would have spared no expense to get the player, or players, the team needed.

Look at what Peter Angelos has done to the Baltimore franchise. Put George there with his mentality, painful as it might be to those who work for him, and he'd win there, too. He's demanding and he drives his people, but he's got his front office constantly on the phone trying to improve the team because they know if they don't they're going to have to answer to him.

I ran into George recently at the summer meeting at Saratoga Race Course and spent some time with him. I was impressed with how informed he is on baseball. Because of the many bad trades he made in the past, he's criticized for having a football mentality and for not knowing baseball. Let me tell you, he knows what's going on. We started talking about the pennant races and George rattled off four or five moves that had been made in the previous few days: "Oakland just got this player, and the Red Sox picked up Cliff Floyd; they're going to be tough. . . ."

I was impressed with how tuned in George is. He's a throwback to the old owners, like Calvin Griffith in Minnesota and Horace Stoneham in San Francisco, whose only business was baseball. George is a combination fan, owner, and sportsman. Some owners, like Tom Hicks in Texas and David Glass in Kansas City, seem to have no clue what's going on in the game. But George is a hands-on owner who makes it his business to know what's happening with the competition.

During the baseball season, I live in a residence hotel in New York City, right in midtown. Every morning I walk down to get my newspaper, and there are always Mets fans and Yankees fans going at each other. One day, a Yankees fan saw me and pointed to a guy wearing a Mets cap. "See that cap?" he said. "The NY stands for 'Next Year.'"

One Mets fan said, "I don't understand it. We're in the same city. We've got access to the same people. Why can't the Mets do things the way George and the Yankees do them?"

It hasn't always been that way. There was a time when the Mets were the glamour team in town and the Yankees were playing catch-up and would have a knee-jerk reaction to anything the Mets did. When the Mets got Bobby Bonilla, George decided he had to have a power hitter to match Bonilla, so he overpaid for Danny Tartabull, who was not the impact player Steinbrenner thought he would be. It was a mistake, one of many mistakes George made in the eighties and early nineties. He acquired high-priced veterans and traded away many of the Yankees' good young players. That all changed when George, to his credit, began listening to his baseball people. It started with Buck Showalter, and it continues to this day.

CHAPTER 16

The Next 60 Years

n more than a half century of following baseball as a fan, a player, and a broadcaster, I have seen many broad and sweeping changes both on and off the field.

I have seen the game expand to the West Coast and grow from 16 teams to 30. I have seen baseball become an almost exclusively nocturnal pastime when, in my youth, it was played mostly by day. I have seen the doors open to blacks and the talent pool increase dramatically with the influx of African Americans, and later with the talented Dominicans and other Latinos, and, still later, with the arrival of players from Australia and Japan.

I have seen the minimum salary for a major league player rise from $4,000 a year to $300,000, and the highest-paid player's salary soar from $60,000 annually to $25 million.

I have seen teams consistently draw 3 million fans in a season. I've seen one player break Lou Gehrig's supposedly unbreakable consecutive-game playing streak, and three players surpass baseball's most cherished record—Babe Ruth's 60 home runs in a season, once thought to be unreachable.

Records fall, franchises move, standards are altered, human beings grow bigger, stronger, faster. Players are more intelligent and more skillful; they have better equipment, better nutrition, better training methods, better teaching aids, better instruction, better technique. But one thing has remained the same for more than 100 years: the essence of the game itself has not changed.

The distance between bases is still 90 feet, and a ground ball to an infielder still routinely becomes an out. The pitcher's mound remains 60 feet, six inches, from home plate and pitchers consistently throw the ball 90 miles an hour and faster, but batters are nevertheless hitting home runs at a greater rate than ever before.

And baseball is still the greatest game ever devised by man.

What's the biggest change in the game over the last 50 years? To me it's the players: their size, their strength, their speed. They're so much more athletic today. You see a player like Troy Glaus of the Anaheim Angels. He's 6'5", 235 pounds, and he's a third baseman agile enough to make the one-hand pick on a slow roller. In my era, a player at 6'5" and 235 pounds would have been a left fielder or a right fielder that couldn't move three feet. All that kind of player could do was swing the bat—guys like Bob Cerv, Gus Zernial, and even Harmon Killebrew.

With the White Sox, I played with two home-run champions. Bill Melton won the title in 1971 with 33 home runs and Dick Allen won it in 1974 with 32. Nowadays, some players have that many home runs by the All-Star break. People used to get excited speculating about a player who had the potential to hit 20 home runs and knock in 90 runs. That was considered a good year at one time. Today it's ordinary. In 2002 the Yankees had four players that did

A Ballplayer Never Forgets

Baseball players have an uncanny ability to remember little incidents that happened in a game 20, 30, or even 40 years earlier; what pitchers were hit, who hit them, where they were hit. My friends often marvel at my ability to recall minute details of a game I pitched in the sixties and not remember what I had for breakfast yesterday.

I'm not alone. An example: in the early sixties, I hooked up in a game with Robin Roberts, who won 286 games and was elected to the Hall of Fame. He had his best years with the Phillies, and he played for Michigan State, so he was one of my childhood heroes.

Robbie was pitching for Baltimore at the end of his career. I was at the beginning of my career with the Twins. We went to the eleventh inning tied at 1–1, both of us still in the game. I came to bat with a runner on first and one out: a bunt situation. Since I was new to the league, Roberts was not aware that, for a pitcher, I was a decent hitter. Expecting me to bunt, he threw me a nice, high, batting practice fastball and I hit it over the head of the Orioles' right fielder, Jackie Brandt, for a triple. I then scored on a squeeze bunt by Vic Power and we won the game, 3–1.

Some 14 years later in 1976 I was traded to the Phillies, Robbie's original team. That winter the Phillies had a luncheon to introduce me to the media. I was seated at a table set for eight but the chair next to me was vacant. In walked Robin Roberts, and he headed right for my table. I had never met him—had not seen him since the day we pitched against each other 14 years earlier. Robbie walked up to the table, looked at me, and without even saying hello, the first words out of his mouth were, "If I knew you were hitting, I'd have thrown you a slider."

---

that, another who missed by one home run, and a sixth who missed by two RBIs.

There's more speed in today's game. Every team has three outfielders that can run. Look at today's shortstops. In my day the shortstops were smaller men such as Luis Aparicio, Larry Bowa, and Bud Harrelson. Today they're big men like Alex Rodriguez, Nomar Garciaparra, and Derek Jeter. Years ago they would have been outfielders, third basemen, or first basemen. Enrique Wilson, a backup infielder with the Yankees, is as big as Mickey Mantle was: 5'11", 195.

There are more blacks and Latinos playing in the major leagues now, great all-around athletes who were denied a chance to play professional baseball 60 years ago. When the doors opened to them, they brought more speed and more athleticism to the game.

Another major change in the game over the past 50 years has been the designated hitter rule in the American League. I'm a baseball purist. I like the game the way it was originally conceived, without the DH. I wish we had never heard the words *designated hitter*.

I say this knowing full well that I benefited from the DH by picking up a few wins I might not have had otherwise. If you're pitching without the DH and you're behind in the sixth or seventh inning, they're going to get you out for a pinch-hitter. With the DH, you stay in the game and you can end up winning it.

I realize fans would rather see a Dave Winfield or a Paul Molitor or an Edgar Martinez bat instead of some pitcher, but the DH distorts the game. Why would you have two sets of rules for the best game ever created?

What disappoints me about today's players is the *SportsCenter* mentality. It pains me to see players get a base hit and barely touch first base when the outfielder fields the ball. Even Bernie Williams, who is a great young man and a terrific player and always busts it on ground balls to the infield, is occasionally guilty of that. We're in an era where the first thing a guy does when he hits the ball is watch where it goes. You see it time and time again.

What's lost today is the image of Pete Rose rounding first base on a single; you knew that if the outfielder bobbled the ball, Pete was going to be on second. Those are the little things that disappoint me. Today's players, with the ability they have, don't do those little things. They don't run the bases. They don't take advantage of fielders' defensive lapses.

It's not that players aren't spending enough time in the minor leagues learning fundamentals. That's not the problem. The problem is that in the minor leagues, coaches are not demanding that young players learn the proper way to do things. It would take me only one day to teach a young player that if he hits a single to center field, he should keep running until the fielder has picked up the ball and thrown to the cutoff man. And if the ball is bobbled, keep going to second. How difficult is that? But they don't do it.

People look at some of the numbers being put up these days and they think that today's players are as great as Hank Aaron, my all-time favorite player. I don't think you can make those kinds of comparisons. It's a different game today.

I was watching batting practice at Yankee Stadium one day and Bernie Williams was in the cage, batting left-handed. The ball just jumped off his bat, long drives one after another. He hit several balls to the 399-foot sign in left-center field, and I remembered shagging balls out there when Harmon Killebrew, a right-handed power hitter and one of the greatest home-run hitters ever to play, didn't hit them that far. The strength of today's players (whether they're using steroids or not), a baseball that is like a Superball, and bats that are made of better wood: those are the reasons for the increase in home runs.

You have to be careful not to go overboard when you see what today's players are doing. I respect what Mark McGwire, Barry

Bonds, and Alex Rodriguez have done, but to put them in a class with Aaron and Willie Mays—I don't know if I buy that. You can't penalize today's players for playing in an era when more home runs are hit, but by the same token, you have to understand that this is a different era. The game has changed. The emphasis is on the home run. You have to revise your thinking with regard to the accepted standards for star status.

Home-run records today are greatly inflated compared to the Aaron/Mays/Mantle era or the Ruth era. To me, comparing today's sluggers to Aaron the "Hammer," or the Mick, or the Babe is blasphemous.

The comparison that jumps out at me is McGwire's 70 home runs in 1998 and Babe Ruth's 60 home runs in 1927. In 1927, no other team in the American League hit 60 home runs. Three teams hit fewer than 30. For McGwire to do what Ruth did in comparison to the rest of the league, he would have had to hit about 260 home runs.

Even the bats used in today's game are more lethal weapons. Moisture in a bat gives it its weight, so bats are stored in a kiln to remove the moisture. Bats are made out of maple, a hard wood; with the moisture removed, they're just as hard, but they're lighter. That's why these days the ball goes farther and you see many more broken bats. If a hitter catches the ball on the "sweet spot," the ball takes off. If he doesn't get it on the "sweet spot," the bat shatters.

Baseball is constantly legislating against the pitcher and for the hitter. They have shrunk the strike zone and made the low strike practically nonexistent.

Like today's players, the umpires of today are more physically fit, they come up to the major leagues at a younger age, and they have better working conditions. But, unlike the umpires of years past, today's umpires have a shorter fuse. Too many of them are like a street bully who is always looking for a confrontation.

In my day, umpires were like a school principal. They'd let you have your say then say, "OK, that's enough. Any more and I've got to run you."

When I played, Ed Runge was the pitchers' favorite umpire. His motto was: "People don't pay their money to see a batter walk."

My all-time favorite umpire was Nestor Chylak. He was fair and he was consistent. Another favorite of mine was Ed Hurley, who was behind home plate for the seventh game of the 1965 World Series. Eddie always gave me candy when he was umpiring on first base and I was sitting on the dugout steps. His strike zone was the size of a cracker box and I would ask him if I could trade a few pieces of candy for a few more strikes. But he was consistent and you always knew where you stood with him, which is all a pitcher can ask.

Television replays show that today's umpires do well with the side-to-side strike, but they miss the low strike too often. Not as many pitches that are six to eight inches outside are called strikes these days, but they're still not accurate from top to bottom. If you could tape 1,000 borderline pitches from a side angle, I'll guarantee you that from 900 to 950 that are called balls are really strikes. I was watching Game 1 of the 2002 World Series on television and in the first inning, Kenny Lofton, the first batter, took two pitches at the knees that were called balls. I'd bet my 1982 World Series ring that they were both strikes. The reason umpires are missing the low strike, I believe, is that they're looking at where the catcher receives the ball.

I don't believe the balls that are used today are juiced up, they're just made better. They're harder and more tightly wound. Add that to lighter bats with harder wood, bigger and stronger players, smaller ballparks, and expansion, and you're going to see higher scoring games in the future. It's a power game. Fans want to see power pitchers such as Clemens, Schilling, and Johnson, and they want to see home runs. It wouldn't surprise me if some player, in the not too distant future, were to hit 100 home runs.

Another factor is the use of steroids. We'll find out in a year or two, with testing, if steroids are a factor. Until it's been proved, we don't know for sure; but most baseball people, who look the other way right now, think it is.

There are great players in today's game—individuals who could have been stars in any era. But the overall product is not as good. It's simply a matter of numbers. If you want to improve the product, go back to the days when we had two eight-team leagues. Then you'd see the best of the best and you'd see some real baseball.

Of course, it will never happen.

I Don't Buy Bonds

I'm a baseball fan and like any fan, I watched in awe at the power display put on by Barry Bonds in the 2002 World Series. He's the modern-day Babe Ruth. I can't remember another player who has affected the game the way he does. He's so strong and he swings that light bat; teams are afraid to pitch to him.

The World Series was his coming-out party. He got the spotlight and he didn't let the opportunity pass him by.

But I'm more than just a fan. I'm a former baseball player and a working baseball broadcaster, and as such, it's tough to root for him. I've been in the Giants' clubhouse. I've seen Barry. I've tried to have a conversation with him. He ignores me. And not just me—he ignores almost everybody.

If I met him when he was a six-year-old, he probably would have jumped into my arms. Now, I can't even get him to talk to me. It's disappointing to me that he won't even acknowledge former players, that he won't show his respect for those who helped pave the way for him. It's a shame he's not a more engaging person. He would be on top of the world if he were.

I pitched against Barry's dad. Bobby Bonds was a talented player, but he could be belligerent, so I can see where Barry gets that. But Bobby could be charming, too. I haven't seen that side of Barry.

I would love to have had the opportunity to pitch against Barry. It would really have been exciting to see how I could have done against him. It would be a great challenge. As a competitor, you enjoy the challenge of going against the best. It always got my competitive juices flowing when I pitched to Ted Williams and Mickey Mantle.

Barry comes to bat wearing all that armor on his right elbow, but pitchers still don't challenge him. They don't try to knock him off the plate. They don't try to make him uncomfortable.

That's how I would pitch him: high and tight, low and away. I can understand managers walking him because when you pitch to him, he's going to kill you. But before I walked him, I would first want to see if I could get him out. That, to me, would be the ultimate challenge.

Baseball went a little crazy with expansion because the owners liked the money they got from the new franchises that came into the game. The down side to that is that they don't have as good of a product as they once did. Many of today's owners are not born competitors; they're bottom line guys. If you give them an additional $50 million, as they did with the latest labor agreement, they're going to stick $30 million in their pockets and $20 million into the team, and that's not the answer. That's not going to improve their team enough to compete with George Steinbrenner.

It's not my intention to trash Bud Selig. He's a nice guy and he has a passion for the game. But people are making him into a hero for saving baseball by getting an agreement before there was a strike. Baseball people will tell you that if it had been left to Paul Beeston, the former CEO of baseball, they would have had an agreement a year earlier. With an agreement in place, attendance in 2002 would have been greater, especially in the month before the deadline. By waiting so long to negotiate a deal Selig hurt baseball—he didn't help it.

This was especially true in Minnesota after Selig let it be known that he was advocating "contracting" two teams out of baseball. It was an open secret that the two teams he was fingering were the Twins and the Montreal Expos. Faced with the prospect of supporting a lame duck team, Twins fans stayed away from the Metrodome, especially early in the season. The Twins got off to a great start and kept it up all season, eventually winning the American League Central Division title. They created enough excitement to draw 1.9 million people. But the Twins figured Selig's threat of contraction cost them another half million in attendance.

I don't see this agreement as the answer to what's wrong with the game. It seems to me that the main objective was to get as much of the Yankees' money as they could get. Taking the Yankees' money doesn't force the Kansas Citys and Milwaukees to do any better. They're welfare recipients. And it doesn't slow the Yankees down. You don't slow George Steinbrenner down by taking his money. He wants to win. Taking his money only gets his competitive juices flowing and he's going to spend more money to win.

If you want to compete with George Steinbrenner, here's the way to do it. Somebody has to be able to go to baseball and say, "I want to put a stadium in Brooklyn and move the Expos to Brooklyn and compete with the Yankees." You would hire the best baseball people, bring in top players, and make it more attractive to watch the

Brooklyn team than the Yankees. If you did that, you would attract your share of the television audience and of the marketing. Right now, baseball protects the territorial rights of its major league teams, so they'd have to change the rules for this scenario to be possible. But it would be for the good of the game.

The Mets are in the Yankees' backyard. They have the same television market, they have access to the same people, but they don't run their organization as well as the Yankees do. That's the key to competing with George Steinbrenner: putting together a good organization—not revenue sharing. The way to level the playing field is to allow more teams to get into big markets.

It stands to reason that if there were only one McDonald's in the city of New York, it would make a killing, wouldn't it? Right now, the Yankees are the McDonald's of major league baseball.

I learned this from Marvin Miller, the former executive director of the Major League Players Association, who is the genius behind the enormous strides players have made over the years in salaries, benefits, and working conditions. Marvin lives a few blocks from where I stay in New York, and one of my great pleasures during the baseball season is to get together with him several times for lunch or dinner. He remains as sharp as ever. He's been retired for almost 20 years and one of my biggest disappointments with today's players is that many of them don't give public recognition to Marvin and how much he's done for them.

As an example of the changing economy in baseball, sometime toward the end of the 1982 season I was approached by a representative of the Pony Shoe Company and asked if I would wear their shoes. There would be a small remuneration in it for me if I did. I explained that I wouldn't wear a new pair of shoes in a game until I had had about a week or two to break them in. I was given several pairs of Pony shoes and I wore them during workouts to break them in so they would feel comfortable during a game.

As the season was ending, and the Cardinals were about to clinch our division title, Pony made me an offer. If I wore their shoes in the National League Championship Series, they would pay me $2,500. If we won the pennant and I wore the shoes during the World Series, I would be paid an additional $2,500. And if we won the World Series, I would get another $3,000. As it turned out, we swept Atlanta in three games in the National League Championship Series. I never got into a game. Then we beat Milwaukee in seven games in the World Series. Of the ten games in the postseason, I got into four of them, a total of two and one-third innings. And for wearing their shoes (mostly on the bench, in the bullpen, and in pregame practice) Pony paid me $7,500. It was more money than I made in my first year in the major leagues.

Now that they have a new four-year agreement and we don't have to worry about labor problems in baseball until 2007, I think it's time for both Bud Selig and Don Fehr, the current executive director of the Major League Players Association, to step down and turn it over to new leadership—two new people who could promote the game and encourage its growth. For years baseball has been one of the few businesses in which owners knock their own product. It happens with arbitration. Management will go before an arbitrator and downgrade its own players in order to sign them at a cheaper price. Then, once that player is signed, management has to build him back up to get the people to come out and see him play. That's like an automobile manufacturer saying, "My people are building the worst car in the world." Why would you buy that car?

Even though the television ratings would not be as high, I also wish baseball would return the World Series to the afternoon so that kids, the paying fans of the future, will be able to watch the games and their interest in the game will be stimulated.

All this may sound like I'm pessimistic about the future of baseball, but I'm not. I'm optimistic about the future. People still love the game; they still want to see it. You hear that kids today don't play baseball, that they're not interested in the game. I don't buy that. I look around the stands and there are many kids at the ballpark, there are thousands playing baseball. There are more kids today, and even though they're also playing other sports such as football, basketball, and soccer, they're still interested in baseball.

The best story I can share to prove baseball's popularity is this: I broadcast a game between the Yankees and the Detroit Tigers late in the 2002 season. It was a meaningless game played in bad weather between one team, the Yankees, that had already won its division title, and another team, the Tigers, that was at the bottom of its division. Yet there were 31,000 people in the stands. When I won my first major league game against Whitey Ford in Yankee Stadium in 1960, there were 3,700 people in the stands. That tells you that teams do a better job of marketing today. They have promotions and premium days and star players, like Derek Jeter and Alex Rodriguez, who are more visible. As a result, it's a more popular game.

I see no reason why baseball, which has been around for more than a century and which has consumed me for the past 60 years, cannot continue to be an attractive game for at least the next 60 years . . . and beyond.

From the time I was seven, I dreamed about being a big-league ballplayer. I made it. I pitched for 25 years in the major leagues, and I'm still pitching behind the mike. I consider myself fortunate to have had such a great vocation. I mean *vacation*!

Appendix

Newspaper Coverage
of Jim Kaat's Career

Legion Stars Win District Title, 4–3

Kaat Rams Homer; Van Dyke's Single Does It in Ninth

Little Jim Kaat was a big gun for the Holland Legion All-Stars Wednesday night.

He pitched a three-hitter and blasted a game-tying home run as the Stars beat a similar team from Grand Rapids, 4–3, to win the District 5 championship at Riverview Park.

The title broke a long jinx for the Holland Stars, who have lost two straight to the Grand Rapids aggregation for the past three years.

But after a long, uphill battle, Holland had a second victory to go with Tuesday night's 7–4 decision. That meant the title in the two-out-of-three series.

The Stars will travel to Battle Creek Monday for the zone play-offs. Holland plays at 9:30 Monday morning and at 2:30 Monday afternoon.

Wednesday night Holland picked up only two hits, but that pair won the game.

Kaat's home-run blast over the right-field fence came in the eighth with Holland trailing, 3–2. In the ninth Ron Van Dyke ripped out a single to score Jack Faber, who had walked along with Bob Woodall.

All three of the Grand Rapids hits were extra-base blows, but Kaat was tough when it counted.

Grand Rapids pitcher Len Holstege was wild in the second so Holland picked up a pair of unearned runs. But despite those three walks, Holland couldn't have scored without three costly errors by shaky Grand Rapids fielders.

Terpstra tripled for Grand Rapids in the bottom of the second and came home on a fly to narrow the count to 2–1.

Grand Rapids went ahead, 3–2, in the bottom of the seventh when a double, triple, and error by Holland's catcher produced two runs.

But when Kaat laced one out on Columbia Avenue it was all tied up. That set the stage for Van Dyke's crucial single in the ninth.

The linescore:

Holland: 020 000 011—4–2

Grand Rapids: 010 000 200—3–3

—The *Holland Sentinel*

Washington Signs Jim Kaat, Outstanding Zeeland Player

ZEELAND—Jim Kaat, former Zeeland High and Hope College baseball star, has been signed by the Washington Senators of the American League.

Kaat, a southpaw who gained all-Kenewa conference honors in his junior and senior years at Zeeland High and was voted to the all-MIAA team in his freshman year at Hope, will begin his professional baseball career with Superior of the Class D Nebraska state league. Kaat is property of the Class A Charlotte team of the Southern Atlantic League, which purchased his contract from the parent club.

After considering offers from five major league clubs, Kaat signed the Washington contract because of a shortage of left-handers in the Senators' farm system.

Jim Winecek of Kalamazoo, scout for the Senators, after watching Kaat in MIAA action, took the big left-hander to Chicago in a recent White Sox–Senator series and had the Zeeland lad perform before Washington manager Cookie Lavagetto and pitching coach Walter Beck. A contract followed.

Kaat, who led the Zeeland Chix to a Kenewa title in his junior year with a 6–0 record and three one-hit wins, sparked Hope College to a runner-up berth in the MIAA this season, compiling a 6–0 record and averaging 12 strikeouts per game with an earned run average of less than two runs. He also posted an 11–12 record with the strong Southwestern Michigan League last summer as a member of the Zeeland Chix.

Eighteen years old, 6'3", and weighing 195 pounds, Kaat will finish the season with the Nebraska club on Labor Day. He will resume his studies at Hope in September. Kaat is the son of Mr. and Mrs. John Kaat of Zeeland.

—The *Zeeland Record*

Cookie's Kitty Is Star Southpaw of Future

Though he is just another one of the Senators' losing pitchers at the moment, Jim "Kitty" Kaat has been receiving glowing tributes around the American League. The highest praise of all, however, comes from the tall southpaw's own manager.

"Kitty should be the best left-hander in the league in a couple of years," Cookie Lavagetto predicted yesterday at the Stadium. "Another Spahn. I'm going to give him every chance to become it. That's why I left him in so long last night. I can afford to be patient. Maybe a top club like the Yankees would have yanked him quick."

THE 21-YEAR-OLD rookie wasn't relieved in the four-run Yankee sixth inning until he had given up a home run, a triple, walked three, and hit two batters.

"He still needs to get his feet on the ground," Lavagetto added. "He's got all the stuff . . . good sinking stuff. His record shows good enough control, too. But right now he lets things bother him. Then he starts pressing and gets wild. Like what happened after Mantle led off the inning last night with the home run."

Ralph Houk, the Bombers' temporary manager, noted that Kaat seemed very nervous "but he is a real good prospect."

WHAT IMPRESSED Ellie Howard most was how hard the lefty threw the ball and what he did with it to a right-handed batter. "He has a good pitch to a right-hander," Howard said. "It looks like it is coming in on you and then it jumps away."

A native of Zeeland, Michigan, Kaat spent one year at Hope College before signing with the Nats. Most of his shortened collegiate career was devoted to lifting weights in order to regain the coordination he lost in a three-month stretch following graduation from high school. In this period he sprouted from 5'10½" to 6'3". He is now 6'4".

THIS IS HIS fourth season in organized ball. His best was 1958 when, with Missoula, he led the Class C Pioneer League in just about everything. In compiling a 16–9 record, he struck out 245 and walked 118. A year ago, when he was hampered by a "knot" in his side, he was 8–8 with Chattanooga and 0–2 with Washington.

—The *New York Daily News*
Dana Mozley

Kaat Wins First Game in Majors

Kaat Hurls Seven Innings; Beats Yanks

Jim Kaat had a lifelong dream fulfilled Wednesday in the most famous baseball stadium as he chalked up his first major league victory—in New York's Yankee Stadium.

Dreams of recording a pitching victory in the major leagues have been primary in Kaat's mind since he began playing catch as an elementary school pupil with his father, John Kaat, in Zeeland.

The dream continued while toiling at Zeeland High School and later at Hope College and kept growing during his three season in the minors.

He had two setbacks last season in the last couple of months of the baseball campaign as he made a bid with the Washington Senators and concluded the season with an 0–2 mark.

Kaat, who was 21 last November 7, had his first start of the season last Thursday before being lifted for a pinch-hitter in the eighth and gave up only three hits. Four runs in the Washington portion of the eighth gave the Senators a 5–4 win and Kaat his first victory.

Kaat walked two and struck out four. The Zeeland lefty retired the first 10 Yankee batters in a row and then the Yanks scored three unearned runs in the fourth. With one out, Gil McDougald singled for the first hit. Bill Gardner then errored on Mickey Mantle's grounder and New York had two men on. After Yogi Berra walked to load the bases, Kaat let go with a wild pitch, scoring McDougald.

An intentional pass to Bill Skowron was followed by Elston Howard's sacrifice fly and Tony Kubek's run-scoring single.

The lone earned Yankee run was gained in the seventh when Skowron homered to give New York a 4–1 lead.

Whitey Ford, one of the game's great southpaws, was sailing along smoothly with a three-hitter when the Senators struck. Ken Asprominte batted for Kaat and flied out. But that was the last man Ford retired.

Gardner bunted safely, advanced to second on Dan Dobbek's infield single, and scored on Bob Allison's single. Ford, who hadn't gone more than seven innings all spring, then pitched to Jim Lemon and Lemon cracked a three-run homer into the lower left-field stands to give the Senators a 5–4 lead. Don Mincher, rookie first baseman, had homered in the third for the first Washington run. Lemon and Skowron each hit their third homers. Ramos relieved Kaat in the eighth and was nicked for two more singles in the frame but got Yogi Berra to foul out with the potential tying run on third.

Only 3,745 fans witnessed the game in the big baseball stadium but it was still Yankee Stadium and a win for Kaat.

—The *Holland Sentinel*

Jimmy Kaat of Zeeland Beats New York Yankees

Rookie Star Gives Three Hits in Eight Innings

NEW YORK, April 28—Big Yankee Stadium didn't scare Jimmy Kaat, the Washington rookie from Zeeland, Michigan, by way of Hope College. He pitched the Senators to a 5–4 win Wednesday and gained the victory over the veteran Whitey Ford.

Washington (5–5) tied the A's for third with a four-run eighth inning, capped by Jim Lemon's two-on homer against loser Whitey Ford (1–1). Rookie Don Mincher also homered for the Senators, who have beaten Ford only twice in 17 decisions going back to 1954 and only five times in 26 decisions during the southpaw's nine-year career.

Left-handed rookie Jim Kaat gained his first major league victory with help from Pete Ramos. The Michigan-reared Kaat allowed just three hits (one Bill Skowron's solo homer in the seventh), walked two, and struck out four before being lifted for a pinch-hitter in the eighth. The Yanks got their other runs, all unearned, in the fourth on two singles, the walks, a wild pitch, and Elston Howard's sacrifice fly.

—The *Kalamazoo Gazette*, April 28, 1960

Quite a Day for Kaat

Smash Costs Kaat
Two Front Teeth

Jimmy Kaat of Zeeland, pitching for the Minnesota Twins, has something to moan about and something to cheer about in a day of mixed emotions Tuesday. Manager Ralph Houk of the New York Yankees named Kaat to the American League All-Star Team for battle with the Nationals in Chicago next Monday. But Tuesday night against the Tigers Kaat was felled by a hot smash off the bat of Bubba Morton, loosing two teeth in the process. Kaat stretched out on the mound as Rich Rollins and Zoilo Versalles rushed to help him. He had to retire from action after the accident in the sixth inning.

—*The Grand Rapids Press*, July 25, 1962

186

Tigers Finally Top Twins

MINNEAPOLIS (UPI)—The biggest Tiger of them all, owner John Fetzer, was on hand Tuesday night and his once-docile Detroit team roared and defeated the Minnesota Twins for the first time this year, 4–3.

Fetzer watched the proceedings from the press box and the Tigers came through when they had to. Their recent skid has seen them drop 9 of their last 12 games. Fetzer obviously wanted to see what was wrong.

And he couldn't find too much to complain about.

Rocky Colavito looped a two-out, tie-breaking single in the top of the ninth to bring in pinch-runner Frank Lary with the winning run. It marked the first win against the Twins in seven games this year.

Cash Slaps Homer

The Tigers went into the eighth inning trailing 3–2 and Norm Cash slapped his 27th homer of the season into the right-field bleachers to knot the score.

Vic Wertz, pinch hitting for pitcher Jim Bunning, who worked the first eight innings, singled in the ninth to start the Tiger attack rolling. Lary went in to run for Wertz and Jake Wood advanced him

187

to second with a sacrifice. Mike Roarke then flied out and Al Kaline drew a base on balls.

This set the stage for Colavito's heroics. The Italian strongman had fouled out in the seventh with the bases loaded, but this time he came through. Terry Fox took over the mound chores for the Tigers and saved the night, striking out the side, the last two men with the tying run on second.

Kaat Loses Teeth

Bunning, in his eight-inning stint, gave up 10 hits. He notched his 10th win of the season to go with 6 losses. He also struck out 10.

Twins' pitcher Jim Kaat of Zeeland, Michigan, was struck in the mouth with a line drive from the bat of Bubba Morton in the seventh. He had a 3–2 lead at the time but left the game, bleeding badly.

As it turned out, he lost two teeth and suffered a cut lip but was reported in good condition.

—*The Grand Rapids Press*, July 25, 1962

Fast-Working Kaat Confuses Hitters

CHICAGO—One of the fascinating and perhaps most significant baseball stories of the year concerns Jim Kaat, a 36-year-old left-handed pitcher with the White Sox. Kaat has had remarkable success with a quick delivery that will probably be copied and that could have an evolutionary effect, lessening the time required to play nine innings.

Kaat has been pitching without a windup since the beginning of the season, and more important, takes as little time as possible between pitches. The fact is, he hurries and works at a feverish pace—sometimes delivering a new pitch every seven or eight seconds. The hitters have no chance to dig in against him, or take practice swings. The instant they step into the batter's box, they must be ready, because Kaat has begun his motion and the ball is on its way.

Some batters, among them Reggie Jackson of Oakland and Bill Freehan of Detroit, have complained about this near-frantic pace. They have hurled angry words at Kaat and have also appealed to the umpires, contending they are the victims of a quick pitch, which is illegal. But by mid-August, Kaat had yet to be charged with a quick pitch, though in a typical game he may throw as many as three pitches that are not allowed because the batter has safely retreated from the batter's box.

FREEHAN TRIED to slow Kaat's pace July 18 in Chicago when Kaat beat the Tigers in one hour and 53 minutes. It was Kaat's fourth complete game that required less than two hours. Freehan repeatedly asked the plate umpire to inspect the ball, knowing full well that Kaat has never been accused of doctoring the ball. Freehan also stepped in and out of the batter's box, feigning dirt in his eye, etc.

Finally, Freehan took his place and hit a foul grounder that he partially ran out. But instead of returning directly to the plate, Freehan chose a circuitous route that took him to within a few feet of Kaat.

Kaat, a stolid Dutchman, couldn't suppress a smile.

"You know all the tricks don't you?" Kaat said to Freehan, not in anger but in admiration.

"Yeah, and I've got one more," Freehan replied.

Freehan continued to the batter's box, and—oops—he stumbled, and accidentally kicked dirt on the plate, necessitating still another delay.

KAAT WON that game, 4–0, one of the few times he didn't require late-inning relief help. This victory made him the American League's first 14-game winner. Eight days later, in Oakland, Kaat became the league's first 15-game winner and again went the distance in a 5–2 triumph. This game was also rapid, requiring one hour and 51 minutes.

Slugger Jackson, who had beaten the White Sox the night before with a four-hit salvo that included two doubles and a thirteenth-inning homer, tried to stall in the second inning, his first time at bat. He repeatedly stepped out of the box and spoke to both Kaat and the plate umpire. It was obvious Jackson was upset. Kaat proceeded to retire Reggie on all four trips to the plate. Only once did Jackson hit the ball out of the infield.

"I admire him for it," Jackson told reporters later. "I think maybe he's quick-pitching, but the umpires say no, so I guess it's all right. Anyway, I don't throw any cuss words at him. Heck, I admire Jim Kaat."

Minutes later, newsmen carried Jackson's words to Kaat.

"He said that?" Kaat asked with a smile.

"He sure did. He said he admires you."

I'M SURE HE didn't really mean what he said," Kaat replied. "If you were on the field and had heard the words he said, you wouldn't guess admiration."

Kaat lost his two starts and didn't win again until almost two weeks after, in Comiskey Park, when he again went the distance in an 11–1 victory over the Angels. Three of Kaat's pitches were not allowed by umpire Russ Goetz because the batter either had stepped out or wasn't in the box.

Kaat stopped the Angels with a five-hitter, didn't permit any stolen bases, and gave up only one hit after the third inning. The time was 2:09, eight minutes longer than Kaat's average for a nine-inning game. After the game the flow of praise from the enemy club-house continued, this time from Dick Williams, the California manager.

"I wish I had him," said Williams. "He's a great competitor and a credit to baseball. There should be 25 competitors like him on every club. Then they could really call it major league baseball."

THE VICTORY OVER, the Angels game could be regarded as a typical Kaat performance. This correspondent, using a stopwatch, clocked Kaat's time on the mound, as well as that of his opponents. The clocking began with the first pitch in each half inning and ended with the third putout. Kaat was on the mound for a total of 35 minutes and 40 seconds, compared with one hour and 14 minutes for his opponents.

The following table reveals the minutes/seconds breakdown, inning by inning.

	Kaat	Opponent
First Inning	7:00	17:34
Second Inning	2:09	14:29
Third Inning	3:41	6:01
Fourth Inning	3:53	10:45
Fifth Inning	7:29	8:30
Sixth Inning	2:27	4:18
Seventh Inning	3:54	2:54
Eighth Inning	3:04	9:25
Ninth Inning	2:03	n/a

Kaat had five perfect innings—the second, fourth, sixth, eighth, and ninth. The only two innings in which he took more than four minutes were the first (7:00) and the fifth (7:29). The Angels scored their only run in the first. In the fifth they loaded the bases on two walks and a single but were unable to score.

The Angles used three pitchers, all of whom worked at what could be regarded as normal speed. Manager Williams made one pitching change in midinning, in the fourth, when Mickey Scott came on in relief of Dick Lange. The fastest inning by an Angel pitcher was the 2:54 in the seventh by Chuck Hockenberry.

THERE HAVE BEEN many effects of Kaat's speeded-up delivery, some unexpected, but at least one could have been anticipated. There have been times when his opponent, subconsciously or otherwise, also quickened his pace.

"I noticed in a Detroit game against Vern Ruhle, when he shut me out, 2–0," Kaat said. "We played that in 1:35—fastest game played this year. After about the third inning, he was getting the ball and throwing it almost as quickly as I was."

To speed up, however, the pitcher must be working in concert with his catcher. Kaat has two sets of signs with his catcher, Brian Downing, one that Downing gives in the traditional squat and another that he flashes before he has taken his position behind the plate. Kaat estimates that 35–40 percent of his pitches are on signs given to him while Downing is upright.

It is a fact that fielders are usually sharper when playing behind a pitcher who doesn't dawdle. Kaat has found this to be true. The White Sox invariably play excellent defense when he is on the mound.

"WE HAD KIND of a humorous situation when I first started," Kaat said. "One day I threw a pitch and Bill Melton [the White Sox third baseman] still had his back to the infield. The previous pitch was a foul ball and he hadn't gotten back to his position.

"I threw the pitch and the next thing I knew, it was right at Melton, but he turned around in time and threw the guy out. So I've had to check my fielders more carefully than I have in the past. Anyway, I think they appreciate it when I work fast. It keeps them on their toes."

Kaat also has discovered that his control has improved. He now throws fewer pitches.

Also, there is considerably less agonizing on what pitch to throw.

"I used to be the kind of pitcher who would try to analyze each situation and think of the very best pitch to throw and where to throw it. When you do that, you leave yourself open to too much second-guessing of yourself.

"Now I find, with this quick pitch, that I get the ball and I have the pitch in mind. Your mind just tells you, 'Fastball, low and away,' and you get the ball and you throw it, 'Fastball, low and away.' Or you think, 'Slider, up and in,' or 'Fastball, up and in.' And I go at it. I hit the strike zone more and I don't leave myself open for second-guessing myself."

THIS DOESN'T MEAN that Kaat always throws the correct pitch.

"I lost a game in Anaheim the other night," he explained. "I had a two-run lead in the ninth inning, two men on, had the hitter 0-and-2, and he tagged a high slider for a hit.

"Later, I thought if I had taken more time, maybe I would have thrown a better pitch, but then I had to tell myself that's not my game. My game is challenging the hitter, being aggressive, and working quickly, and I don't think you can ask yourself to do both."

Kaat was regarded as over the hill when the White Sox acquired him on waivers from the Twins in August of 1973, certainly one of the more fruitful waiver transactions in recent years.

Kaat had won only 10 games in 1972 and his 15–13 record in 1973 didn't indicate progress. So, early in the 1974 season, he and Johnny Sain, the White Sox pitching coach, began discussing ways he could improve.

"I just felt I had lost the zip from my fastball," Kaat said.

Sain, who had been Kaat's pitching coach for two years at Minnesota, suggested a quicker release, the theory being that the quicker the arm movement, the quicker the ball moves. It required a considerable change in Kaat's delivery. He previously had a long and somewhat deliberate motion. Indeed, a check of the records revealed that in 1965 (when he was 25–13 with Minnesota) the average time for his 19 complete games was 2:24, near the league average.

THE DECISION was made for a compact, no-wind delivery. Kaat tried it for the first time in Cleveland on June 18, 1974. He went the distance in a 7–3 victory, the 200th of his major league career. The time of the game was 2:12. Kaat continued using this new style, finished the season with a remarkable 21–13 record, and this past spring decided he would carry the no-windup to the extreme and throw every pitch as quickly as possible.

As soon as he received the ball, he would step on the rubber and fire. He now can do this with such speed that the batter must be prepared for a pitch every eight or nine seconds, unless he fouls off the previous pitch.

It wasn't until the third week of the 1975 season that he began to realize one large, unanticipated bonus—the hitters didn't like it because he was catching them unaware and off-stride.

By mid-August, Kaat had pitched nine complete games in which the average time was two hours and one minute. That's 25 minutes below the league average.

Said Kaat with a laugh: "I can win 'em fast. And I can lose 'em fast, too."

—*The Sporting News*
Jerome Holtzman

White Sox's Big Winner Using Kaat-Quick Pitch

The scouting report on Jim Lee Kaat is uncomplicated. He's a 6'4" (despite the bowlegs), 36-year-old aspiring sportscaster who spends the winter playing golf at Errol Estate and the summer pitching baseball games like he left the motor running.

The quick-pitching central Florida resident also spends a lot of time lateraling off all the accolades to his Chicago White Sox teammates and to the hurry-up style that is propelling him to a second straight 20-win season. Like Tuesday afternoon, for example, just hours before he would face the Kansas City Royals in pursuit of victory number 20 of 1975.

"When I started the quick-pitch style last spring, the original purpose was to get a quicker release, a quicker spin, and more stuff on the ball," Jim said by long distance. "It did all of that, but there have been two important by-products. The guys seem to play better behind me because it keeps them on their toes, plus I've found that the hitters aren't really ready for it."

Indeed, frustrated American League hitters must think Kaat is trying to make the 9:00 movie. He gets his signal, then fires without benefit of a wind-up. The instant he gets the ball back from the catcher, he's ready to go again.

I have it on good authority that Jim accidentally stumbled onto this method one day when he forgot to go to the bathroom between innings.

Anyway, the result has been not only red-faced rival batters, but ambushed fans, teammates, and even umpires as well. Chisox third-sacker Bill Melton vows he'll never again aimlessly watch another foul ball into the stands and get surprised by a hot grounder a flicker of an instant later. That happened one night when Kaat was racing through one of his frequent sub-two-hour games. (One lasted only an hour and 35 minutes.)

Several of the men in blue admit more than one Kaat delivery has caught them daydreaming. And any fan who allows his wife an extra 15 minutes in front of the mirror when Jim is scheduled to start runs the risk of walking in on the bottom of the sixth inning. A guy foolish enough to visit the restroom with Kaat working may emerge only to find the stadium dark and empty. A trip to the concession stand only costs him two innings.

Opposing hitters haven't taken too kindly to Kaat's methods. Especially Oakland's controversial slugger Reggie Jackson, who was fanned by Jim in one recent game before he hardly got his bat off his shoulder. Reggie dug in, tapped the plate with his bat, and looked up just in time to see strike one whistling by. When he looked back to complain to the ump, the count leaped to 0-and-2.

"Then I tried to throw him a real quick one and got away with it for strike three," Kaat recounted. "It frustrated him so much, he started screaming and hollering at me."

What did Reggie scream and holler?

"I don't think you could print it."

Oh.

Kaat also credits much of his smiling summer to Chisox reliever Rich Gossage. "I've lost three or four games that I could have won, which would have put me well over 20," says the winningest active American League hurler. "But by that same token, Rich has saved a lot of games that quite possibly I wouldn't have won. So I could have won as few as 13 or 14 at this point.

"Twenty is just a number and there's really too much importance put on it. Whether I had won 20 or not doesn't make me that much better a pitcher."

The White Sox, who have relished Jim's late-career comeback, would probably disagree. And they no doubt also hope Jim is not really serious when he says he might retire after this season.

"I'd like to look into the possibility of announcing or maybe explore some avenues in the Orlando area this winter. You'd like to quit while you're somewhere near the top and yet it's hard to turn your back on the financial rewards," said Kaat, who is drawing a six-figure salary in his third season with Chicago, his 17th in the majors. "I played in Minnesota for practically nothing for so many years. Now to be in a position to recoup a lot of that in a short period of time is kind of attractive."

It would also be fun to get another crack at the All-Star Game, in which Jim set down all six National Leaguers he faced this summer.

"It was a fun thing because I was anxious to see how some of their hitters would react to my new quick motion. Johnny Bench kidded me at the luncheon that day that he wasn't going to be fooled by it."

Sure enough, after Lou Brock became Kaat's second out that night, the ball was whipped around the infield and delivered back to Jim. Kaat wheeled around and quickly toed the rubber only to discover Bench already in the batter's box with his lumber posed and a broad grin plastered across his face.

—The *Holland Sentinel*
Larry Guest

Ageless Kaat a Vital Link in Card Bullpen

ST. LOUIS—As much as anything, the bullpen was responsible for the St. Louis Cardinals' fastest start in years.

In Bruce Sutter, the Redbirds were getting what they paid for, even though manager Whitey Herzog still didn't think Sutter was as sharp as he has been or will be. Sutter had eight saves and a victory in 16 appearances and had lost a lead only once. On a swing through Houston and Atlanta, Sutter had three saves and a win, accounting for all the Cardinals' victories, although he needed exceptional defensive plays by first baseman Keith Hernandez in two of the games.

Herzog speculated that Sutter's rhythm was still slightly ajar. "He looks like he's going too fast at times," said Herzog.

There is the natural tendency to expect so much from Sutter because he has been productive in his previous five seasons.

"Everybody expects me to strike everybody out," said Sutter after giving up two runs before he saved a 4–3 victory over Atlanta. "I don't know about that stuff. I don't want to hear about it. I don't worry about it."

But consider this. Sutter had 8 saves in a month. The Cardinal bullpen had only 27 all last year.

If the Cardinals are getting good mileage out of Sutter, they are getting more to the gallon than they could have expected out of 42-year-old Jim Kaat, who has become the left-handed foil to Sutter.

Kaat gave up only one run in 13⅔ innings in his first 10 games in May. He had saved two games and won two, despite being confined largely to middle relief.

In Sutter's save against the Braves, Kaat had rescued the Cardinals from a bases-loaded predicament in the sixth inning when he inherited a 2–0 count on Rafael Ramirez. Kaat threw two pitches. The first was called a strike and on the second, Ramirez grounded out to end the threat.

Kaat, in one stretch of three innings, threw three double-play balls. "That young kid can do it," said third baseman Ken Oberkfell.

Winner of 273 games in his career, Kaat obviously has seen plenty of starting duty. "Any pitcher who's not a short reliever like Goose Gossage or Bruce would rather start, but I understand what my role is," said Kaat. "Whitey made that clear from the very beginning. When the phone rings, you just about know what's going to happen.

"It's a tougher job for me than starting in terms of margin of error. Bet there are probably as many rewards. You're in like a minigame. You can throw three pitches and throw the whole game away. Or you can throw three pitches and contribute to a win."

Through May 24, Kaat had appeared in more games (17) than any other Cardinal pitcher.

"I'm not concerned about how many days I can pitch in a row. Usually when I get up in the bullpen, I get into the game. Sometimes I might only throw four pitches. I'm never in there long enough to be taxed," he said.

—The *St. Louis Post-Dispatch*
Rick Hummel

Cards' Jim Kaat Bearing Down on Milestone for Longevity

ST. PETERSBURG, Fla.—Whoever said life begins at 40 wasn't a baseball player.

There are only a half dozen of the graybeard set, among 650 major league players, who have defied the more than 100–1 odds to duel Father Time to a standoff.

Probably the most remarkable of all the "over-40 crowd" is Jim Kaat, a 43-year-old southpaw who works out of the bullpen for the St. Louis Cardinals.

"I've been fortunate," says the big fellow they call the "Kitty Man" for two reasons—his name and the fact that he seems to have nine lives. "I've been blessed with a durable arm and a durable body. I haven't had any major breakdowns."

To give you an idea of how long Kaat has been pitching in the majors, ask a small fry fan if he's ever heard of the Washington Senators. No? Well, Kaat broke into the big leagues with the Senators in 1959.

He is beginning his 24th year in the majors, his 26th in baseball, and is bearing down on a milestone for longevity. When he pitches in his first game for the Cardinals this spring, he will set a major league record for most years pitched—24. He is presently tied with Early Wynn at 23.

He had his best years with the Minnesota Twins from 1961 into 1973, hitting his high in 1966 with a 25–13 record, one of his three 20-win seasons.

Kaat is slim and trim. There are no bulges on his 6'4", 195-pound frame.

He was 6–6 with the Cardinals last season with a 3.40 earned run average. He's already worked in five spring games for the Redbirds, posting a 2.70 ERA.

What makes Kaat stand apart from his other two grizzled pitching contemporaries—Phil Niekro and Gaylord Perry—is that he still relies on his fastball to get batters out. He says he throws it 75 percent of the time.

Niekro is a knuckleballer whose pitch requires little effort to throw and causes no wear and tear on the arm. Perry has been accused forever of throwing a spitball, which doesn't put much pressure on a pitcher's arm.

"Naturally you lose some pop on your fastball as you grow older," Kaat concedes, "but the secrets are the spin you put on the pitch and its location. Where you really lose it as you get older is on your sharp-breaking pitches. You can't snap them off like you once did."

In his heyday, Kaat said he had a live sinker, a fastball, and a good breaking pitch.

"I've tried to come up with different pitches over the years," Kaat said of his battle with age. "I've worked hard on perfecting a better change-up, and throw a palm ball every now and then. But basically, I'm still a fastball pitcher."

Kaat says he can pitch every day under certain conditions. "When you come in and throw only eight or ten pitches, you can come right back and do that several days in a row. When you go in there for three or four innings, it takes something out of you. But I think you could say that about any pitcher, not only us old timers." Kaat says he arrives for spring training and does "a lot of throwing" to get ready.

He says he hasn't eaten a steak or prime rib for seven or eight years. He says he also stays away from sugar and salt.

"Meat is tougher on your digestive system," he says, explaining his diet. "Every time somebody has a circulatory or heart ailment, one of the first things the doctors do is take them off red meat.

"I'm not fanatical about meat," he adds. "If I go to a friend's house for dinner and he has meat in a stew or something, I'll go ahead and eat it. I merely stay away from meat as much as I can."

In the winter, Kaat returns to his farm in Glen Mills, Pennsylvania, near Philadelphia, where he breeds standardbred horses.

He said Del Miller, one of harness racing's all-time great drivers, got him interested in the business. "He got [ex-Yankee great] Charley Keller into the game, too," Kaat explains, "and I hope to do as well as Charley has."

What does St. Louis manager Whitey Herzog think of his ageless lefty?

"He's something else," cracks Herzog. "He's the only guy on a pension who is still playing."

From his viewpoint as the voice of experience, Kaat thinks the 1982 Cardinals have a legitimate shot at the National League East pennant.

"There is great balance in the division," Kaat points out. "Whoever wins it might not have to finish too many games over .500. It looks like everybody is capable of beating each other.

"But these guys [the Cardinals] don't have to have 'great' years to win. They only need normal, productive years, everyone doing his job.

"This club has a lot of the ingredients of a championship team."

How long will Kaat, who says he's never lost his love for the game, continue pitching?

"I'll keep running out there [to the mound] until the hitters start beating my brains out. Then I'll go running back to the farm. They'll tell me when to quit."

—The *Evansville Courier*
Bill Fluty, *Courier* Sports Editor

Jim Kaat Survives with a Smile

The most durable pitcher in the history of major league baseball, entering his 25th season, is on Key Biscayne this week for some fun and sun and to pick up a paycheck from ABC-TV. He is an entry in the Superteams competition, to be filmed today and tomorrow, for a Sunday broadcast.

It's hardly a serious occasion, this tug-of-war between the St. Louis Cardinals and the Washington Redskins, winners of the World Series and the Super Bowl.

But it is the time of year for Jim Kaat to be serious, so when he came to Miami yesterday from the St. Louis spring-training encampment in St. Petersburg, he brought his baseball glove.

"I'm just going to go out and throw some with [St. Louis pitcher] John Stuper," explained Kaat after being asked why he was carrying his glove aboard a Sonesta Beach hotel elevator early yesterday afternoon. "The weather was bad in St. Petersburg Saturday and Sunday and I couldn't throw. I can't afford to miss throwing for three days in a row in February.

"Business first, pleasure later."

Most of the major league pitchers and catchers check into their training camps later this week. Kaat, 44 years old and convinced that he can pitch indefinitely, has been throwing in Florida since February 1. He is the early bird of the Cardinals.

If Kaat gets through the 1983 season and wins a roster spot at the start of the baseball year in 1984, he will have played major league baseball longer than any man in the history of the game. With 24 consecutive seasons, he has already played longer than any other *pitcher*.

Kaat goes so far back that as a kid he pitched against Ted Williams and Stan Musial. Deciding that he was finished, the Minnesota Twins gave up on Kaat 10 years ago. Since then, the Phillies and the Yankees have ripped uniforms off his back. But Kaat pitched well enough last year to win five games (losing two) for the team that won the World Series.

Kaat's motto has become a rallying cry for all aging athletes who refuse to go down and stay down: "I'll never be considered one of the all-time greats, or even one of the all-time goods. But I'm one of the all-time survivors."

There was a time when bitterness might have touched Kaat's outlook. "It's tough to love the game after it has stopped loving you," he said back in the seventies when a team shoved him aside. But now the 6'5" left-hander has a smile on his face. "I take pride in being a survivor," he said.

Kaat has won 283 games, a lot more than many pitchers who are in the Hall of Fame. It is unlikely that his uniform will ever go to Cooperstown, because he has lost 233 times. Kaat has played for too many losing teams.

But he has an upbeat philosophy about that, too: "Maybe there ought to be a Hall of Achievement for players who did quite a bit but were not so famous because they weren't in so many World Series. And if there is a Hall of Enjoyment, I'm in it right now. Pitching in the World Series again last year was the epitome of the Hall of Enjoyment."

Kaat pitched three games for the Twins in the 1965 World Series. He had to wait 17 years to get back into the finals of baseball's play-offs once more.

In his first major league season, with the Washington Senators in 1959, Kaat made $6,000. Last year he earned upward of a quarter of a million dollars for pitching just 75 innings, and got a World Series ring and a bonus, too.

If baseball's big salaries had come along 15 years ago, Kaat would have been a $1-million-a-year pitcher, as so many are now. Because he started at $6,000, and appreciates what has happened in recent years, Kaat is not envious at all. "It's impossible for younger players to comprehend how well they have it," he said.

Baseball has tried to get rid of James Lee Kaat, who won 13 straight Gold Gloves as the best-fielding pitcher in his league, many times. He simply refused to go.

Minnesota dumped him in 1973. He won 21 games for Chicago in 1974 and got 20 more for the White Sox the following year. Philadelphia decided he was through in 1979. The New York Yankees didn't want him any more after the 1980 season.

St. Louis grabbed Kaat and has been bringing him back on one-year contracts ever since. His three-year record for the Cardinals is 19–15. He even started a game for Whitey Herzog last year, went six innings, and got credit for the victory. Almost all of his work has been in relief. "An occasional participant, more of a spectator," is how he described his role with the Cardinals.

But he certainly is not ready to leave baseball. "Why would you want to quit on top," he asked, "unless you were independently wealthy?

"I'm the walking answer to trivia questions," said Kaat.

Sample: Name seven players who have played major league baseball in four different decades. Answer: Kaat, Early Wynn, Ted Williams, Minnie Minosa, Tim McCarver, Mickey Vernon, and Willie McCovey.

Not bad company for a guy who lost seven of his first eight decisions when he came to the major leagues.

Kaat makes light of any questions about whether he deserves to be in the Hall of Fame. "I'm laughing with tears in my eyes," he said with a grin. "But at my age, when you do just a little bit, you get a lot of everything. You get exposure, money, and recognition. How can I complain?"

—John Crittenden, Sports Editor

He's Just a 44-Year-Old Kid

Jim Kaat Refuses to Let the Midlife Crisis Get Him Down

ST. PETERSBURG, Fla.—The fresh-faced kids in the Cardinal clubhouse who treat him with a distinct reverence were not on this earth when, as an 18-year-old hayseed, he came to his first spring-training camp in 1957.

But Jim Kaat, 44 years old, is really one of them—a kid and a ballplayer.

While many people his age are frantically trying to cope with that frightening fifth decade, Kaat refuses to let midlife crisis tie him in knots. He doesn't even know what it is. When you are forever playing, life never seems to progress in stage.

"Anyone playing this game is a kid, basically," said Kaat, who in stature (6'5") and demeanor is very much *not* a kid.

Kaat had just returned from a Busch complex practice field here where he is developing an underhanded pitch.

After 874 major league games (only four pitchers have appeared in more), Kaat is working on something new. And this surprises no one.

"His competitiveness and the intensity inside him wear off on other people," pitcher Dave LaPoint said. "Just being around him you know you should be doing something to improve yourself."

Manager Whitey Herzog was a player at that Washington Senators spring camp 26 years ago.

"He [Kaat] was a country boy who was wilder than a March hare," Herzog remembered.

The Senators were never much of a team but they did have some big-name players.

"I remember being in awe . . . of Roy Sievers, Jim Lemon, Camilio Pascual, and Pedro Ramos," Kaat said. "It was a feeling of intimidation."

Perhaps the same intimidation some of today's 20-year-old Cardinals feel in the presence of Kaat?

"I don't think the young players today feel that as much," he said.

"The big-league players are so much more visible now through TV. When I was a kid [in Michigan] I followed the Tigers. We'd drive to the games but you could never tell what the players looked like. You saw their pictures in the paper occasionally but you didn't see them in person."

* * *

Kaat is working his left arm on a stretching device he keeps in his locker.

Sitting in front of the locker next to Kaat's is Jerry Garvin, a new Cardinal who pitched six seasons with the Toronto Blue Jays. Garvin, a 26-year-old left-hander, has, according to Herzog, a chance to replace Kaat this season.

Knowing that this man is his competition, Kaat shows Garvin how the stretching device works.

"If you ever want to use this, you can," Kaat tells him.

Typical Kaat. Never hesitating to help a young pitcher, always enthusiastic.

"I ask his advice," says John Stuper. "Who else are you going to go to around here for the ins and outs of the game?

"I have two idols—Tom Seaver as a right-handed pitcher and him as a left-hander. I hope I can have anywhere near his enthusiasm in just five years."

But Kaat doesn't force his ideas and his experience on Stuper or anyone.

"I enjoy a relationship with a young pitcher, one who cares about improving himself," Kaat said. "With Stuper and John [Martin] and David [LaPoint] we talk about pitching and that's enjoyable for me."

Says LaPoint: "He keeps us going and we keep him going." Kaat says that once he's in the clubhouse or on the field, "I'm not treated like I'm any particular age. We're all just ballplayers."

* * *

Kaat is the leader of the team's exercise sessions here, twisting and stretching his body, keeping it free of bulges. The only bulge is the one in his cheek where he stuffs a wad of Red Man chewing tobacco.

"I'm not as much into physical fitness programs as people think I am," Kaat said. "I'm just interested in keeping my body in shape. I've always stayed active in the off-season."

His diet is fat-free. Seven years ago he started avoiding red meats, sugar, and salt.

"Instead of a hot fudge sundae I'll have a cup of yogurt," he said. "I stay away from candy and sweets."

Pitching coach Hub Kittle is an admirer of Kaat's physique. "He's gifted with a very, very loose body," said Kittle. "He has a soft arm like mine. Here, feel mine, it's like jelly."

After practice, Kaat puts on a white Dallas Cowboys T-shirt and gray shorts and rides a stationary bicycle until sweat appears on his face, a face made prominent by a good-sized nose and remarkable by a shortage of lines.

"He enjoys this game, he really does," says Herzog. "He enjoys his chewing tobacco, riding that bike, and spinning yarns to the young pitchers."

If it's early morning, hours before the 10:00 A.M. practice, Kaat is usually one of the few players present. If he's not, you can expect Herzog to say, "Eight forty-five . . . I can't believe he ain't here yet."

Kaat enjoys romping around the outfield after balls during batting practice. It's called shagging.

"He tries to catch every ball that's hit near him out there," says Kittle. "He's a tremendous fielder, quick like a cat."

Kaat doesn't let shagging or any of the other mundane rituals of spring training get boring.

"This is a serious business to me," he says. "I'm out here trying to make a living, but I still want to have fun doing it."

* * *

It is cold as Kaat starts pitching to Darrell Porter. He is trying his new underhanded delivery. The ball is rising wickedly as it nears the plate. On a day like this, it would be dreadful for any left-hander to try to hit it.

"I'd never like to hit against him," says Porter, who batted against Kaat when both were in the American League.

"He's so deceptive. The ball gets on you so much quicker than you think it's coming."

Left-handed and underhanded. The combination has probably never been seen in baseball before. Kaat played with a couple of right-handed "submariners" with the Senators—Dick Hyde and Ted Abernathy.

Normally a sidearmer, Kaat doesn't look at this new gimmick delivery as something that will extend his career even further. He is more concerned with using it to get left-handed batters out in important situations in 1983.

The various pitches Kaat will throw off his new delivery, in Herzog's opinion, can be effective for getting that one big out and "if I don't show [pitch] him too much."

Kaat admits he has benefited from the scarcity of left-handed pitchers in recent years. Would he still be pitching if he were a right-hander?

"No," says Herzog.

* * *

Over Kaat's 23 big-league seasons he says there have been two big changes in the game: speed and short-relief pitching.

And, of course, money.

"We used to fantasize about making $50,000," he said. A big fantasy, considering that Kaat's first-year salary was $6,000.

"Then, all of a sudden it was $100,000. And then we sat around in the late sixties wondering if someday someone would make $200,000 playing this game. And then Dick Allen did."

And now, 24 years after his six grand, Kaat himself is a $200,000 ballplayer.

"I'm the first to admit that comparing what we do against hard labor, we're all overpaid," he said. "But this shows you how much revenue is generated by TV. If the owners could not afford to pay these salaries, the teams would fold."

To anyone's knowledge, no player has ever held a gun to the head of a general manager or owner.

"Years ago you'd try to pump yourself up to the general manager, sell yourself to get more money and they'd try to cut you down. Today they open their checkbooks and there it is."

—The *St. Louis Globe-Democrat*
Dick Wagner
Tuesday, March 1, 1983

Kaat Reluctantly Ends His "25-Year Vacation"

The telephone rang several times before Jim Kaat finally answered, an indication that the veteran pitcher was not perched by it night and day waiting for a major league baseball club to call, offer work, and end his apparent retirement.

"I don't feel like I am physically washed up," said Kaat from his farm in Glenn Mills, Pennsylvania. "What I have done is run out of opportunities."

Kaat, released by the St. Louis Cardinals after a career that spanned a record 25 seasons, has been unable to strike a deal with another team.

"I guess I've turned the page on my playing days," said the 44-year-old Kaat, who was the second oldest active pitcher before being cut by the Cardinals July 6. "I had a 25-year vacation. I have no complaints.

"I am not going to come out and say I'm glad it's over. I wish I was still playing.

"And I'm not considering myself a retired baseball player," said Kaat. "If someone gets into dire straits, calls, and offers an opportunity to play, I'll play. I can still turn the page back. But being realistic, I have to think those chances are quite remote."

"I wouldn't want to stay in baseball just to establish any individual records," said Kaat, 17 victories short of 300. "That's not the purpose of the game. I feel I've been a contributor on every team I've played for."

Kaat said he didn't expect his baseball career to end so abruptly.

"They gave me my unconditional release, which is baseball's polite language for saying you are fired," said Kaat. "It happened so fast, with no warning, it was a shock and traumatic for the first few days. But I'll look elsewhere, either broadcasting or breeding horses.

"I'd be interested in coaching in the right situation. But I really think my future is in broadcasting," said Kaat, who worked for ESPN during the 1981 baseball strike. "If I could work out a deal to help a club instructing younger pitchers and do some broadcast work, that would be ideal."

Only one active pitcher is older than Kaat—by 22 days—and that is Gaylord Perry, who was signed by Kansas City after being dropped by Seattle a month ago.

Kaat, a three-time 20-game winner with a career record of 283–237, was released when the Cardinals acquired Dave Rucker from the Detroit organization. Rucker, also a left-hander, was born in 1957, the year Kaat began his professional career.

When St. Louis released him, Kaat said he would look for a club with a shortage of left-handed hurlers and made some calls. But he was turned down by Milwaukee, the Chicago White Sox, and Pittsburgh.

"They have younger pitchers in the farm system they want to bring up," he explained.

"I had Dick Moss [an agent] make some inquiries for me but there wasn't any interest," said Kaat. "What hurt me is that St. Louis is supposed to be looking for pitching. So other clubs have to wonder why did the Cardinals get rid of me. I was also looking for a contract for 1984, not just to finish up this season."

Kaat started 625 games, sixth on the all-time list. He broke in with Washington in 1959 and moved to Minnesota (where he won a career-high 25 games in 1966), Chicago (winning 21 games in 1974 and 20 in 1975), Philadelphia, and the New York Yankees before becoming a Cardinal in 1980.

Last year he became the first man to pitch in 24 major league seasons, appearing in 62 games for the world champions. That marked the most appearances he had in any year. He was in 24 games this season, his 25th, and 898 for his career—the fifth highest number in major league history. His victories rank him 19th on the list and his 2,461 strikeouts are the 18th highest, right behind Don Drysdale.

There are other distinctions. Kaat was one of only seven men to play in four decades. The others are Willie McCovey, Mickey Vernon, Ted Williams, Early Wynn, Minnie Minoso, and Tim McCarver. He had 16 home runs, tops among active pitchers starting this season, and won 16 consecutive Gold Gloves between 1962 and 1977.

"I'm approaching life like my playing days are in the past," said Kaat. "I'm comfortable with that. But one thing I've learned in this game is never to say never. I would never want to shut the door and say there is no way I would ever play again."

—The *Minneapolis Star and Tribune*
Dan Stoneking, Staff Writer
Wednesday, July 20, 1983

This report included information from the Associated Press.

Kaat's Career Statistics

Table Key

IP = Innings Pitched

SO = Strikeouts

W = Wins

L = Losses

ERA = Earned Run Average

Year/Club	IP	SO	W	L	ERA
1959/Washington[1]	5	2	0	2	12.60
1960/Washington	50	25	1	5	5.58
1961/Minnesota	201	122	9	17	3.90
1962/Minnesota	269	173	18	14	3.14
1963/Minnesota	178	105	10	10	4.20
1964/Minnesota	243	171	17	11	3.22
1965/Minnesota	264	154	18	11	2.83
1966/Minnesota	305[2]	205	25[2]	13	2.74
1967/Minnesota	263	211	16	13	3.05
1968/Minnesota	208	130	14	12	2.94
1969/Minnesota	242	139	14	13	3.50

Year/Club	IP	SO	W	L	ERA
1970/Minnesota	230	120	14	10	3.56
1971/Minnesota	260	137	13	14	3.32
1972/Minnesota[3]	113	64	10	2	2.07
1973/Minnesota-Chicago[4]	224	109	15	13	4.38
1974/Chicago	277	142	21	13	2.92
1975/Chicago[5]	304	142	20	14	3.11
1976/Philadelphia	228	83	12	14	3.47
1977/Philadelphia	160	55	6	11	5.40
1978/Philadelphia	140	48	8	5	4.11
1979/Philadelphia[6]	8	2	1	0	4.50
1979/New York[7]	58	23	2	3	3.88
1980/New York[8]	5	1	0	1	7.20
1980/St. Louis	130	36	8	7	3.81
1981/St. Louis	53	8	6	6	3.40
1982/St. Louis	75	35	5	3	4.08
1983/St. Louis	34⅔	19	0	0	3.89
American League totals	3,699	2,175	237	191	3.31
National League totals	828⅔	286	46	46	3.97
Major League totals	4,527⅔	2,461	283	237	3.45

World Series record

Year/Club	IP	SO	W	L	ERA
1965/Minnesota	14⅓	6	1	2	3.77
1982/St. Louis	2⅓	2	0	0	3.86
World Series totals	16⅔	8	1	2	3.78

Holds World Series records for most putouts by a pitcher in a seven-game series (five, in 1965) and most putouts by a pitcher in nine innings (five, on October 7, 1965).

1. Signed as a free agent by the Washington Senators organization on June 17, 1957.
2. Led American League.
3. On disabled list, July 6 to September 27, 1972.
4. Sold on waivers to the Chicago White Sox on August 15, 1973.
5. Traded with shortstop Mike Buskey to the Philadelphia Phillies for outfielder/infielder Alan Bannister and pitchers Dick Ruthven and Roy Thomas on December 10, 1975.
6. Sold to the New York Yankees on May 11, 1979.
7. Granted free agency on November 1, 1979; re-signed by the Yankees on April 1, 1980.
8. Sold to the St. Louis Cardinals on April 30, 1980.

—*The Sporting News* Baseball Register

Kaat Eyes Future
After His Release

ST. LOUIS (UPI)—His bags were packed, but Jim Kaat had nowhere to go. "I'm heading to a telephone to contact some other teams to see if there's any interest," said Kaat, standing before his suitcase yesterday in the St. Louis Cardinals' clubhouse at Busch Stadium.

After 25 years in baseball, the Glenn Mills, Pennsylvania, resident is without a team. The Cardinals asked waivers on him Wednesday for the purpose of giving him his unconditional release. Other teams have until Monday to nab Kaat from the waiver list.

"I'd like to pursue it, but I'm realistic enough to know that at my age teams aren't going to be knocking my door down."

If there is no interest, a career that spanned four decades will close quietly.

"It's really not that important except from a personal challenge standpoint," Kaat said of his efforts to put off his end. "If I felt I couldn't throw the ball anymore or had an injury, I'd say forget it."

Kaat began his professional career in Superior, Nebraska, in 1957. He joined the Washington Senators in 1959, but spent most of his years with the Minnesota Twins, leading them to their last American League pennant in 1965 when he had an 18–11 record.

Kaat won a career-high 25 games the next season for Minnesota, and won 21 with the Chicago White Sox in 1974 and 20 the next season. He also played with the Philadelphia Phillies and the New York Yankees before joining the Cardinals in 1980.

Kaat appeared in a personal-high 62 games as St. Louis won the world championship last year. But he had no record in 24 relief appearances this season and a 3.97 earned run average.

"If you're 24 and you get batted around, they say, 'He'll come around,'" said Kaat. "When you're 44, they say you're out of it."

Kaat said at a news conference he would contact the Chicago Cubs and the Pittsburgh Pirates to see if they're interested in a veteran left-handed reliever.

"I knew one of these days that bullet would hit me. But I can't really show any signs of disappointment because of the good things that have happened in the last 25 years."

Kaat, who won 16 consecutive Gold Gloves from 1962 to 1977, appeared in 898 games pitched 4,528 innings, and recorded 283 victories. He is the only pitcher in major league history to appear in 25 seasons.

Kaat said Al Kaline was the best "pure hitter" he faced in his career, and listed free agency, artificial turf, the emphasis on speed, and the importance of the short reliever as the greatest changes in the game.

"The thing I miss the most—if I don't play anymore—are the things that go on in the clubhouse," said Kaat. "The relationships between the players and coaches. Those are the things that are unique to the life of a ballplayer."

Index